SpringerBriefs in Economics

More information about this series at
http://www.springer.com/series/8876

Norbert Gaillard

When Sovereigns Go Bankrupt

A Study on Sovereign Risk

Springer

Norbert Gaillard
Economist and independent consultant
Corbeil-Essonnes
France

ISSN 2191-5504 ISSN 2191-5512 (electronic)
ISBN 978-3-319-08987-4 ISBN 978-3-319-08988-1 (eBook)
DOI 10.1007/978-3-319-08988-1
Springer Cham Heidelberg New York Dordrecht London

Library of Congress Control Number: 2014943914

Printed on acid-free paper

Springer is part of Springer Science+Business Media (www.springer.com)

Abbreviations

BIS	Bank for International Settlements
CAC	Collective action clause
CDS	Credit default swap
CFB	Corporation of Foreign Bondholders
CRA	Credit rating agency
ECR	Euromoney Country Risk
FBPC	Foreign Bondholders Protective Council
FC	Foreign currency
GDP	Gross domestic product
GNP	Gross national product
ICRG	International Country Risk Guide
IMF	International Monetary Fund
LC	Local currency
MIGA	Multilateral Investment Guarantee Agency
NYSE	New York Stock Exchange
OECD	Organization for Economic Co-operation and Development
OTC	Over-the-counter
S&P	Standard & Poor's
SCDS	Sovereign credit default swap
WEF	World Economic Forum

Contents

Introduction

In the sixteenth, seventeenth, and eighteenth centuries, sovereign states borrowed to wage war but then would sometimes refuse to honor their financial commitments, plunging merchants and bankers into bankruptcy. With the advent of the *Pax Britannica*, relationships between creditors and debtor states evolved and became less inimical to investors. The defeat of Napoleon at Waterloo ensured the military, economic, and financial supremacy of Great Britain and paved the way to a century of peace. Under the auspices of the Rothschilds, *haute finance* played a key role in the prevention of major wars and in the spread of capitalism. As Polanyi (1944) explains:

> *Haute finance* functioned as a permanent agency of the most elastic kind. Independent of single governments, even of the most powerful, it was in touch with all; independent of the central banks, even of the Bank of England, it was closely connected with them. There was intimate contact between finance and diplomacy; neither would consider any long-range plan, whether peaceful or warlike, without making sure of the other's goodwill.

From the 1820s through 1913, London-based banks (e.g., Rothschild, Goldschmidt, Baring, and Hambros) lent extensively to European countries and newly independent Latin American nations, thus boosting foreign government bond markets. Inevitably some states defaulted, but in general they were under severe pressure to repay their debts. Creditors might wield their diplomatic influence or rely on the Corporation of Foreign Bondholders (CFB), established in 1868, to press their claims. More subtly, bankers could serve as lenders of last resort in convincing recalcitrant debtors to resume payments. More roughly, they could persuade the British government to employ gunboat diplomacy; this approach was in line with Lord Palmerston's circular of 1848, which asserted the right of the state to use force in order to recover foreign government debts.

Military interventions against insolvent countries (e.g., the British intervention in Egypt in 1882; the blockade of Venezuela in 1902 by Great Britain, Germany, and Italy) were on questionable grounds because they infringed upon the rights of sovereign nations. The threat of such coercive measures was lessened by the Drago–Porter Convention of 1907, which prohibited the recovery of sovereign debt by force *unless* the debtor state refused arbitration, prevented any workable compromise, or (after arbitration) did not submit to the award. Arbitration was the conventional means of settling debt disputes until the shift to national courts that began in 1945 (Waibel 2011).

Since 1815, the relationships between sovereign debtors and private creditors have been increasingly based on the rule of law, and also states have become more accountable for their debt policy. These trends have been reinforced since the 1970s for several reasons. First, the restrictive approach to sovereign immunity – which distinguishes between acts of government and acts of a commercial nature – has gained ground in Western countries and has thus discouraged governments from not honoring their financial obligations. In the United States, for example, the Foreign Sovereign Immunities Act (FSIA) of 1976 allows investors to sue a foreign government in US courts if the complaint relates to commercial activity, which includes sovereign debt (Delaume 1994). Second, the prominent role played by the International Monetary Fund (IMF), especially since the 1980s, has enabled low- and middle-income countries to avoid default (although the financial facilities offered have been conditional on specific macroeconomic policy commitments; Boughton 2001). Third, the growing public debt in both industrialized and developing economies has obliged governments to launch active debt management strategies and has motivated investors to strengthen their monitoring.

However, that creditor-friendly path has not prevented some major defaults. From this viewpoint, many valuable lessons can be learned from the recent Greek sovereign debt crisis. Most economists, financial analysts, and policy makers failed to anticipate the economic debacle of the Hellenic Republic. In November 2008, few weeks after Lehman Brothers collapsed, the country was still rated in the single-A category by major credit rating agencies (CRAs) and the Greek–German 10-year bond spread was no more than 160 basis points (Gaillard 2011).

By late 2009 and early 2010 – that is, once the severity of the crisis was recognized – European governments seemed helpless and diverged on how best to cope with it. Was a bailout package really necessary? If so, then what was the appropriate amount to provide? Should the IMF be involved? If so, then what type of austerity measures should be implemented? Shortly after the support package – offered by the European Union (EU) and the IMF – was announced in May 2010, it became evident that Greece's public debt was unsustainable. The key issue was then to organize the debt restructuring and to divide the burden between private and official creditors. In February 2012, private bondholders "voluntarily" accepted a nominal haircut amounting to 53.5 % of the face value of Greek sovereign securities; at the same time, EU member states agreed to a new loan at a lower interest rate.

What has transpired since this agreement was reached? On the debtor side: Greek unemployment has continued to rise, driving young workers to migrate; austerity measures have undermined the legitimacy of the political system; and the ratio of public debt to gross domestic product (GDP) has stabilized – albeit far above the 150 % threshold, which calls into question how stable the situation can remain in a deflationary context. On the lender side, private investors suffered losses, yet official creditors (European taxpayers in essence) may end up paying much more in the event of an additional restructuring.

The idea behind this SpringerBrief originates in the "lose–lose" situation just described. More precisely, the purpose of this monograph is to provide a fresh analysis of how to cope with sovereign risk in the context of a rising likelihood of default. Chapter 1 identifies the different forms that a sovereign default may take, and Chap. 2 surveys how creditors traditionally seek to protect against sovereign risk. Chapter 3 focuses on policies implemented by creditors to prevent a state bankruptcy. Chapter 4 assesses the determinants of sovereign creditworthiness.

Chapter 1
Identifying Sovereign Defaults

Abstract Chapter 1 examines the key concepts used throughout the book. This chapter discusses why the notion of "creditworthiness" is better suited than those of "solvency" and "bankruptcy" for explaining sovereign risk and goes on to show that the risk of sovereign default depends on the country's ability *and* willingness to pay. Next, Chap. 1 investigates the various policies that a borrowing state may implement to alleviate its debt burden. These policies include repudiation, missed payment, moratorium, unilateral and negotiated restructuring, exchange control, and special tax on bonds. Debt repudiation has historically put creditors in serious jeopardy (e.g., Mexico in the last third of the nineteenth century and Russia in the aftermath of the Bolshevik revolution). Yet forced debt restructurings, lengthy renegotiations, and negotiated restructurings – especially when influenced by political factors – have also led to heavy losses for creditors. Even though it is not tantamount to default, monetary erosion is another major threat to debtholders.

Keywords Sovereign default • Solvency • Creditworthiness • Repudiation • Moratorium • Debt restructuring • Monetary erosion

For a clear understanding of the issue, it is necessary to examine carefully the key notions that will be used throughout the book.

A *sovereign default* is defined as a state's failure to fulfill its financial obligations. According to Borchard (1951, p. 117), such default can be viewed as a breach in the terms of the covenant between the lender[1] and the borrowing state. For Standard & Poor's (2006, pp. 25–26), an issuer's debt is in default under any of the following circumstances.

- For local and foreign currency bonds, notes, and bills: when *either* scheduled debt service is not paid on the due date *or* an exchange offer of new debt contains terms less favorable than the original issue.
- For central bank currency: when notes are converted into new currency of less than equivalent face value.

[1] The terms "bondholder", "debtholder", "banker", "lender", and "creditor" are used interchangeably hereafter.

N. Gaillard, *When Sovereigns Go Bankrupt*, SpringerBriefs in Economics,
DOI 10.1007/978-3-319-08988-1_1

- For bank loans: when *either* scheduled debt service is not paid on the due date *or* a rescheduling of principal and/or interest is agreed to by creditors at less favorable terms than the original loan. Such rescheduling of short- or long-term bank debt is considered a default even when (for legal or regulatory reasons) creditors deem the forced rollover of principal to be voluntary.

For Moody's Investors Service (Moody's 2013a, p. 58), the following types of events are deemed to constitute sovereign default.

- A missed or delayed disbursement of a contractually obligated interest or principal payment as stipulated in credit agreements and indentures.
- A "distressed" exchange, whereby: (i) an obligor offers creditors a new or restructured debt – or a new package of securities, cash, or assets – that amount to a diminished financial obligation relative to the original obligation; and (ii) the exchange has the effect of allowing the obligor to avoid a payment default in the future.
- A change in the payment terms of a credit agreement or indenture imposed by the sovereign that results in a diminished financial obligation, such as a forced currency re-denomination or a forced change in some other aspect (e.g., indexation or maturity) of the original agreement.

Insolvency is the financial state of an entity that "is unable to pay all debts as they fall due", and *bankruptcy* is "the state of a person who has been adjudged by a court to be insolvent". Finally, a *creditworthy* entity is one "considered suitable to receive credit, especially because of being reliable in paying money back in the past".[2]

These definitions raise several problems, but they do reveal the idiosyncratic features of sovereign risk. The concept of *bankruptcy* does not apply to sovereign debt issuers. The reason is that no court is entitled to liquidate a sovereign's assets and its property cannot be formally sequestered or seized. Thus insolvency is synonymous with "state bankruptcy", a term I use in a provocative way for the title of this book. However, some observers argue that a state cannot truly be insolvent because it can always cut expenditures, nationalize private firms, increase taxes, and so forth. This point of view, exemplified by Walter Wriston's claim in September 1982 that countries do not go bankrupt because each owns more than it owes,[3] implies that debtors default "not because they are *unable* to pay all or a good part of their debt service, but simply because they do not have the *will* to pay" (Clark 1940, p. 122; emphasis added). Yet, there are clearly limits to this approach. Even though instances abound of states not making all possible efforts to meet their financial obligations, creditors must be realistic and admit that drastic measures intended to prevent a country's default may trigger political and social unrest. That being said, it is evident that the risk of sovereign default depends both on the country's ability to pay and on its willingness to pay. These factors buttress the

[2] http://www.oxfordreference.com and http://www.oxforddictionaries.com

[3] Then chairman of Citigroup, Wriston was reacting to the default of Mexico.

claim that the notion of "creditworthiness" is better fitted than that of "solvency" for grasping the concept of sovereign risk.

More concretely, a borrowing state may implement various policies to alleviate the burden of its debt. Several different forms of sovereign default are described in this chapter.[4] It is worth remarking that they are far from mutually exclusive – especially when a government would move heaven and earth to avoid fulfilling its obligations.

1.1 Repudiation

Debt repudiation is certainly the most brutal form of default. It "constitutes a refusal to admit the binding character of an obligation" because that obligation is perceived or declared to be illegitimate or illegal (Borchard 1951, p. 129). Repudiations are often related to a revolution or to a succession in state or government. A number of repudiation episodes played out in the nineteenth, twentieth, and twenty-first centuries. Some of the more notable ones are summarized next.

In 1867, in the aftermath of the fall of Maximilian, the Mexican government repudiated two loans because they had been issued for the purpose of fighting the Juarez regime (CFB 1904, p. 259). In 1918, the Soviets reneged on Tsarist debt on the grounds that it was contracted "by the governments of the Russian landlords or of the Russian bourgeoisie" (Taracouzio 1935, p. 250). In November 2008, Ecuador announced that it would not remit the payments due on two USD-denominated bonds – issued in 2000 and maturing in 2012 and 2030 – after an audit found them to be "immoral" and "illegitimate" obligations (Moody's 2013a, p. 12).

Although debt repudiation is not supported by any principle of international law,[5] some theoreticians have argued that it would deserve to be so under certain conditions. Sack (1927) forged the doctrine of "odious debt": following a state succession, a sovereign debtor could repudiate the debts of its predecessor if those debts were incurred against the interests of the population and without its consent (i.e., by a despotic regime) and if the creditors were aware of these conditions. Ludington et al. (2010) challenge Sack's doctrine, emphasizing that the stipulation involving debt contracted by a "despotic" regime does not meet prevailing standards of arbitration decisions and international law. Scrutinizing the *Tinoco*

[4] This typology is by no means exhaustive. Readers will find complementary information in Winkler (1933), Borchard (1951), Wynne (1951), Panizza et al. (2009), and Reinhart and Rogoff (2009) as well as in annual reports released by the Corporation of Foreign Bondholders (1874, 1878, 1895, 1904, 1907, 1943).

[5] However, Borchard (1951, p. 129) states that "repudiation may have a legal justification" if "the loan contract is defective in law, either because there was no constitutional or legislative authority to contract the debt or because in other respects the rules of law governing a binding obligation were not observed."

arbitration of 1923, however, these authors acknowledge that the "odious debt" doctrine could well be reshaped to become an international rule.[6]

Debt repudiation exemplifies the unwillingness of a sovereign debtor to fulfill its financial obligations. Yet with other types of defaults it is even more difficult to distinguish between unwillingness and inability to pay.

1.2 Missed Payments

A less severe form of "bankruptcy" consists of missing a loan or bond payment or missing a scheduled coupon repayment. The default is recorded when missed payments are not "cured" within the contractually allowed grace period (e.g., 30 days). Such defaults are rife in developing countries that experience political uncertainties and suffer from fluctuating revenues.

During its war against Peru and Bolivia of 1879–1883, Chile deferred debt amortization (*Moody's Manual* 1937, p. 2526). In the period 1920–1922, Liberia paid its gold loan coupons with a 12-month delay on average (*Moody's Manual* 1922, p. 395; *Moody's Manual* 1924, p. 515). In 2000 and 2002, Ukraine and Moldova (respectively) failed to honor their obligations at due dates; they rolled over their defaulting bonds into new debt instruments with later maturity dates (Moody's 2013a, pp. 20, 24). These latter two cases show how different sovereign default types may be intertwined: a missed payment may lead to a debt restructuring or a debt moratorium.

1.3 Moratorium

A debt moratorium takes the form of a partial or complete suspension or cessation of debt payments that may apply to principal, interest, and/or amortization. This type of default differs from the previous one in that it often concerns the whole debt (or a nonnegligible portion of it) and reveals the borrower's willingness to reduce debt overhang. A moratorium may (i) be a de facto payment standstill or (ii) stem from a juridical decision (e.g., a law or decree) or an official announcement by the defaulting government.

Debt moratoria are frequent in periods of major financial turmoil. In June 1931, US President Hoover proposed a one-year moratorium on payments of World War I debts. In the meantime, several Latin American countries (e.g., Brazil, Chile, Costa Rica, Peru) suspended the service of their debt denominated in foreign currency

[6] In the *Tinoco* case, Chief Justice Taft stated that Costa Rica was not bound to repay the debt incurred by its former president Tinoco on the grounds that he used the funds for personal purposes, a fact that was known by the creditor.

(CFB 1943, pp. 131, 154, 172, 239). They subsequently resumed partial payment of that debt until readjustment plans were set in the 1940s and 1950s. A similar sequence unfolded when Mexico declared a three-month moratorium on principal payments to its foreign creditor banks in August 1982. Other countries (Brazil, Bolivia, Peru) followed suit, which triggered large-scale debt restructurings involving the IMF, the Bank for International Settlements (BIS), the US Federal Reserve, the Paris Club, the London Club, and hundreds of creditor banks (Boughton 2001, pp. 281–414; Sachs 1986, pp. 424–427).[7] In August–September 1998, Russia and Ukraine declared a moratorium on their foreign currency debt service before they (respectively) restructured their bonds and converted them to local currency as a prerequisite for any repayment (Moody's 2013a, pp. 19–20).

1.4 Restructuring

Debt restructurings include cases where the bankrupt state – either unilaterally or after reaching an agreement with its creditors – scales down the debt's interest rate and/or amount due, extends its maturity, changes its currency denomination, or modifies any contractual clause so that the new conditions are less favorable to the creditor than those previously applicable (see Appendix 1A for the debt restructuring deals reached during the period 1970–2010). Such restructuring is also known as "rescheduling" and "reprofiling". This section focuses first on unilateral and then on negotiated debt restructuring.

1.4.1 Unilateral Restructuring

One type of nonnegotiated restructuring may couple debt adjustments (based on a lower interest rate, a reduction in the principal, and extension of the payback period) with conversion, consolidation, or unification strategies.[8] In 1840, 1845, and 1852, for example, Portugal converted GBP bonds into new bonds with lower interest rates (Wynne 1951, pp. 364–365). Turkey resorted to similar unilateral action during the period 1875–1877 (CFB 1904, pp. 393–396). Unilateral restructuring turned out to be a standard form of debt settlement during the Great Depression. Between 1933 and 1936, the Polish, Spanish, Portuguese, and Czechoslovak governments launched conversion and unification operations that applied

[7] The Paris Club is an informal group of official creditors set up in 1956. The London Club is an informal group of private creditors whose first meeting took place in 1976. The role of these two clubs is to help debtor countries find sustainable solutions to their payment difficulties.

[8] Conversion, consolidation, and unification consist (respectively) of exchanging, consolidating, and unifying the old debt under new terms that are less favorable to creditors (Borchard 1951, pp. 323–324).

to their debt denominated in local currency (BIS 1936, p. 54); the result was a reduction in interest rates by one third on average. In February 1934, a presidential decree provided an adjustment plan involving Brazilian bonds denominated in USD, GBP and French franc. The securities were classified into eight grades: the higher the grade, the higher the interest repaid to creditors (*Moody's Manual* 1937, p. 2100).[9] In July 1940, Colombia established the following basis for a permanent settlement of its USD debt. The two 6 % external US dollar bonds of 1927 and 1928 were converted into new 3 % bonds; 50 % of arrears of interest was to be cancelled and 50 % to be funded into new 3 % bonds and a sinking fund was to be set up and the new 3 % bonds to be redeemed by 1970. This scheme was strongly criticized by the Foreign Bondholders Protective Council (CFB 1943, pp. 166–167). In contrast, there have been only a few forced and strictly noncooperative restructurings of this kind since the onset of widely globalized finance – namely, Peru in 1986 and Nigeria in 1990–1991 (Enderlein et al. 2012, p. 256).

A second type of unilateral restructuring consists of operations that convert foreign currency debt into local currency. Such adjustments offer two advantages: (i) they alleviate the debt burden to the extent that the local currency depreciates against the foreign currency; and (ii) they incentivize debtholders to invest in the debtor country. This option was taken by (among others) Spain, Uruguay, Turkey, and Ukraine in 1901, 1933, 1936, and 1998, respectively (CFB 1943, pp. 262, 284, 269; Moody's 2013a, p. 20).

The last type of unilateral restructuring is bond buyback performed by a defaulting borrower. In "normal times" (i.e., as long as the country respects its financial obligations), this technique is common and typically does not breach any law or contract agreement. But unless it is allowed by the bond covenant, a buyback amounts to a unilateral restructuring once a default has occurred. Repurchasing bonds at discounted prices reduces the volume of the debt to be restructured and reflects the debtor's reluctance to negotiate with its creditors. Several abusive debt buyback operations were conducted in the 1930s and 1940s. Bolivia, Chile, Colombia, and Peru repurchased 5 %, 18 %, 22 %, and 31 % of their outstanding debt in default at discounts of (respectively) 84 %, 41 %, 78 %, and 79 % (Jorgensen and Sachs 1989, pp. 67–68). Although Peru is reported to have conducted buyback operations in 1996 (Enderlein et al. 2012, p. 256), this type of unilateral restructuring seems to have been relatively rare during the past two decades.

[9] A definitive restructuring plan (see Appendix 1B) was set in 1943 following negotiations between the Brazilian government and representatives of the CFB and the Foreign Bondholders Protective Council (FBPC), the American bondholders association.

1.4.2 Negotiated Restructuring

The most noteworthy characteristics of cooperative restructurings are less the measures actually undertaken to reduce public debt[10] than the methods used to induce agreement among debtors and creditors.

The defaults of Central American countries in the second third of the nineteenth century lasted an exceptionally long time.[11] This can be attributed to civil unrest, political and institutional instability, poor economic diversification, and lack of coordination among creditors. Such drawn-out debt disputes were less frequent after the Corporation of Foreign Bondholders was founded in 1868. In its first report, the CFB's council proclaimed its ambition to gather bondholders' claims against defaulted borrowers (CFB 1874, p. 60) as follows:

> Every measure of the Council tends to promote that union of the Bondholders which constitutes a real force against their antagonists. So long as separate action was the rule there was no desire to employ the force of one body of holders against the adverse government of another loan, nor was it indeed possible. It necessarily followed that beyond the Committee of the Stock Exchange, or perhaps the contractor for the loan, a new Committee had no allies and had to enter on its contest with unequal forces. This state of affairs is now undergoing a change.

The initiatives launched by the CFB and its French counterpart (the Association Nationale des Porteurs Français de Valeurs Mobilières, established in 1898) contributed to rebalancing debtor-creditor relationships and shortening the average duration of defaults on foreign government bonds, which fell from 14 years during 1821–1870 to 6.3 years during 1871–1925 (Suter and Stamm 1992, p. 653). However, creditor coordination soon weakened owing to the 1931 financial crisis, the unprecedented number of sovereign defaults, the resurgence of protectionism and nationalism, the exacerbated rivalry among European powers, and the rigidity of the newly created American bondholders association (the FBPC).

After World War II, cooperation between debtors and creditors was reached through innovative ways. In addition to the agreements traditionally sought by bondholders organizations and commercial banks – for example, the belated negotiations to settle Latin American and Eastern European debts in the 1950s and the Brady deals arranged in the 1990s – debt restructurings came increasingly to involve multilateral financial institutions (e.g., the IMF and the World Bank) as well as both Paris Club and London Club creditors. The multilateral approach represented a shift in resolving debt disputes because Bretton Woods institutions

[10] Negotiated or not, a restructuring process inevitably results in an interest rate reduction, an extended maturity and/or a debt exchange.

[11] Upon leaving the former Central American Federation, the countries of Costa Rica, Guatemala, El Salvador, Honduras, and Nicaragua were allotted a portion of the £163,000 loan issued in 1825 by the federation. The debts of the five countries lapsed into default in the late 1820s and were not repaid until 1840, 1856, 1860, 1867, and 1874, respectively (CFB 1904, pp. 100, 186, 330, 219, 284).

have increased their lending arrangements since the 1970s although loans are conditional on fiscal policy adjustments (see Chap. 3 for details). This new debt renegotiation framework has led to a decline in the average length of restructurings: 31 months during 1980–1997 versus only 13 months during 1998–2010 (Das et al. 2012, p. 27).

This evolution does not change the natural reluctance of debtholders to engage in restructuring processes. In some cases, debtholders have been induced by various parties to give their consent. Pressure came from the IMF when Latin American debt was renegotiated during 1982–1989 (Sgard 2012, pp. 19–21) and from European governments when the Greek debt exchange was prepared in 2012 (Eurogroup 2012, p. 2).[12] In other cases, dissenting bankers and bondholders have been tempted to free-ride in order to gain preferential treatment. Such strategies may consist of (i) separate negotiations (CFB 1904, pp. 233–234), or (ii) lawsuits against sovereign borrowers (Gulati and Klee 2001, pp. 1–2), which may affect other lenders.

1.5 Defaults Due to Exchange Controls

Exchange control is mentioned here because it is likely to trigger a default on debts denominated in a foreign currency. This scenario arises when debtors are unable to convert their local currency funds into "the money required by the bond because of lack of foreign exchange normally accruing to them from favorable trade balances, new loans, gold production, or other sources" (Borchard 1951, p. 130).

Exchange controls were widespread during the Great Depression: by 1937, Belgium, Denmark, Germany, Greece, Hungary, Italy, Poland, Yugoslavia, and most Latin American states had imposed such measures to prevent capital flight (BIS 1937, pp. 24–25; Eichengreen and Sachs 1985, p. 928). However, such controls made more sense for an undiversified economy like Chile, whose exports plummeted by 87 % between 1929 and 1932 (*Moody's Manual* 1937, p. 2524), than for Germany, which used its foreign currency reserves to buy military equipment (Borchard 1951, p. 134). In many instances, exchange controls preceded a default or were concomitant with a debt moratorium, thus posing a threat to sovereign solvency.

It is worth noting that the imposition of exchange controls in one country may incidentally lead to the default of another country. In 2002, Paraguay's largest commercial bank – a subsidiary of an Argentine bank – was liquidated after its major shareholder was hit by the deposit freeze and exchange control measures adopted by the Argentine government. In combination with an economic slowdown and narrow foreign currency resources, this "bankruptcy" obliged Paraguay to

[12] The Eurogroup used the term "invitation" when referring to the PSI (private sector involvement) exchange offer.

renegotiate its USD-denominated bonds as early as 2003 (Republic of Paraguay 2013, p. 30).

1.6 Special Taxes on Bonds

Special taxes on bonds are an atypical form of default because they do not fundamentally jeopardize the creditworthiness of the sovereign borrower.

Between the 1880s and the 1930s, the countries of Russia, Italy, Spain, and France levied a tax on the coupons for some bonds held by national residents. In 1868 and 1999, Austria and Turkey (respectively) set a tax on bonds denominated in local currency; this tax affected both domestic and foreign investors (Borchard 1951, pp. 125–126; Moody's 2013a, p. 22). Although a government may argue that such measures are part of its tax policy, they are normally viewed by lawyers, investors, and CRAs as a breach in the bond covenant.

1.7 Monetary Erosion

Monetary erosion is the bane of debtholders but, under the standards of international law, it is not tantamount to default. This is simply because, by the principles of monetary sovereignty, a country's executive or legislative branch holds the exclusive right to issue and regulate the country's currency and to determine its value vis-à-vis other currencies (Waibel 2011, pp. 58–59).

Hence, whether investors purchase bonds denominated in their domestic currency or in a foreign currency, they have no cause of action if their bond holdings are devalued as a result of inflation, hyperinflation, currency devaluation, currency depreciation, or monetary reform. This lack of recourse is a real concern for creditors, who should bear in mind that all major countries in the world recorded at least 1 year of inflation exceeding 16 % during the period 1800–2008 (Reinhart and Rogoff 2009, pp. 184–187).

Today, investors are usually well informed about such risks. For instance, the prospectus that advertises the 8.75 % notes – issued by Egypt in 2007 – denominated in Egyptian pounds and payable in US dollars states that "if the Egyptian pound depreciates against the U.S. dollar, the effective yield on the Notes (in U.S. dollar terms) will decrease below the interest rate on the Notes, and the amount payable on an interest payment date, at maturity or upon acceleration, may be less than a prospective purchaser's original investment in the Notes" (Arab Republic of Egypt 2007, p. 7).

1.8 Creditor Loss by Default Type

Now that the different forms of default have been described, it is time to assess which are the most costly to creditors. Toward this end, two types of indicators are scrutinized: the real rates of return obtained by investors and the haircuts imposed on them in the event of a default. Table 1.1 displays realized real returns on bond lending to ten major sovereign borrowers for the periods 1850–1914 and 1915–1945. Table 1.2 reports the ten heaviest haircuts (in relative terms) experienced by foreign private creditors during 1970–2010.

Table 1.1 Realized real returns on bond lending to ten foreign governments, 1850–1945

		Rates of return (%)			USD mil. at 1913 prices	
Borrowing nation	n	ν	ρ	$\nu-\rho$	*NPV*	L_o
Bonds issued, 1850–1914 (or outstanding in 1850)						
Argentina	113	3.52	1.81	1.71	251.6	928.1
Australia	232	3.02	2.01	1.01	319.2	1,525.2
Brazil	79	2.27	1.38	0.89	1,223.5	841.8
Canada	62	4.77	3.50	1.27	39.9	65.7
Chile	32	2.79	1.31	1.48	55.0	249.7
Egypt	18	6.41	3.49	2.92	222.4	367.9
Japan	32	1.85	0.60	1.25	190.3	914.9
Mexico	37	−0.74	1.98	−2.72	−157.3	475.7
Russia	48	1.31	2.94	−1.63	−691.1	3,340.9
Turkey	42	1.61	3.17	−1.56	−166.9	695.4
Bonds issued, 1915–1945						
Argentina	70	3.34	1.39	1.95	135.3	928.0
Australia	114	4.18	2.97	1.21	279.3	2,165.1
Brazil	64	4.31	3.61	0.70	32.9	436.7
Canada	243	3.41	2.76	0.65	93.9	379.1
Chile	28	0.54	2.44	−1.90	−58.9	251.6
Egypt	3	4.41	5.41	−0.73	−2.9	40.9
Japan	9	5.89	3.62	2.26	83.2	340.2
Mexico	0	0	0	0	0	0
Russia	0	0	0	0	0	0
Turkey	3	−3.16	−2.27	−0.88	−3.4	47.2

Source: Lindert and Morton (1989, pp. 52–53)
Notes:
n = number of bonds covered
ν = internal rate of return implied by the bond issue price and repayment terms
ρ = rate of interest on bond lending to the home government (UK consol rate or US Treasury long-term bond rate, depending on the place of issue)
$\nu-\rho$ = aggregate rate spread
NPV = net present value, defined in the following special way: the amount investors were able to save by buying the same promised repayment stream from a foreign government at higher interest instead of from the UK or US government
L_o = gross value originally lent to the foreign government

Table 1.2 Top ten sovereign debt haircuts, 1970–2010

Country	Date	Debt affected (USD mil.)	Haircut (%)
Bolivia	March 1988	473	92.7
Bosnia and Herzegovina	December 1997	1,300	89.6
Iraq	January 2006	17,710	89.4
Argentina	April 2005	60,572	76.8
Honduras	October 1989	132	73.2
Costa Rica	May 1990	1,384	71.9
Serbia and Montenegro	July 2004	2,700	70.9
Ecuador	June 2009	3,190	67.7
Peru	March 1997	10,600	63.9
Poland	November 1982	2,225	62.9

Source: Author classification from Cruces and Trebesch's (2011) database
Notes: The haircuts are measured in terms of their loss severity percentage. The haircut measure compares the present value of the old debt to the present value of the new debt. Only restructurings with foreign private creditors are studied; foreign creditors include foreign commercial banks (i.e., London Club creditors) as well as foreign bondholders. Restructurings that are donor funded or supported by bilateral or multilateral money are excluded

Many lessons can be drawn from these two tables. First, debt repudiation puts creditors in serious jeopardy: it was the leading cause for (i) the negative realized real returns recorded in Mexico in the last quarter of the nineteenth century and Russia a few decades later and (ii) the haircut that followed Ecuador's default in 2009. Second, forced debt restructurings and lengthy renegotiations often lead to heavy losses for creditors. In the 1920s, the Turkish nationalist government made no effort to reach an agreement on the Ottoman debt (Wynne 1951, pp. 482–518). More recently, Peru and Argentina – in default during 1984–1997 and 2001–2005, respectively – each engaged in unilateral restructuring (Enderlein et al. 2012, pp. 261–262). The third lesson is that even negotiated restructurings may be harmful for investors when they are affected by political factors. In Poland, debt renegotiations took place in the context of the Cold War and while the country was under martial law (Richard Portes, "Declaring Default on the Polish Debt Is Irrelevant", *Wall Street Journal*, 26 May 1982). The Iraq case illustrates the geopolitical motives of a great power like the United States for shielding a debtor from its creditors (Weiss 2006, pp. 5–10). More broadly, the debt relief given to Bosnia and Serbia shows how difficult it is to be repaid by successor states (Stumpf 2010, pp. 309–310; Diaz-Cassou et al. 2008, pp. 50–53). Fourth, in the cases of Bolivia and Costa Rica, debt restructuring was inevitable because of their excessive debt-to-GDP ratio (see Sachs 1988, pp. 711–712 for an in-depth analysis of the Bolivian debt relief).[13] Finally, major "bankruptcies" may occur in countries with poorly diversified economies and thus no alternative but to suspend debt payments when there is a sudden fall in commodity markets. This was the case in Chile and

[13] The notion of debt sustainability is examined in Chap. 4.

Honduras in the 1930s and 1980s, respectively (Pack 1932, pp. 10–22; Boughton 2001, pp. 802–804).

These various default episodes demonstrate that sovereign creditworthiness is a function of political, economic, and financial factors. This realization is crucial for investors who intend to protect efficiently against unreliable and unscrupulous debtors.

Chapter 2
Protecting Against Sovereign Defaults

Abstract Chapter 2 analyzes the various means used by creditors to mitigate sovereign risk well in advance – that is, when countries issue bonds, sign loan agreements, or are at an early stage of their borrowing cycle. Section 2.1 looks at sovereign bond and loan covenants: it presents the clauses that enable creditors to enforce contracts, secure repayment flows, avoid subordination, neutralize the risk of repayment on unfavorable terms, obtain specific guarantees, and make debt renegotiations easier once a default has occurred. The main provisions studied here are the choice of law, arbitration, currency, pari passu, and collective action clauses (CACs) as well as pledges, negative pledges, and "inflation-proof" clauses. Section 2.2 addresses the various insurance and insurance-like instruments that investors can rely upon to hedge against default risk; these include sovereign risk insurance covenants, contracts of guarantee offered by multilateral agencies, and credit default swaps (CDSs).

Keywords Sovereign immunity • Collective action clauses • Pari passu • Hedging • Insurance contracts

This chapter examines the various means used by creditors to mitigate sovereign risk well beforehand – that is, when countries issue bonds, sign loan agreements, or are at an early stage of their borrowing cycle.[1] Section 2.1 looks at sovereign bond and loan covenants: it investigates the clauses that enable creditors to enforce contracts, secure repayment flows, avoid subordination, neutralize risk of repayment at unfavorable monetary conditions, obtain specific guarantees, and make debt renegotiations easier once a default has occurred. The provisions studied here include primarily choice of law, arbitration, currency, pari passu, and collective action clauses (CACs) as well as pledges, negative pledges, and "inflation-proof" clauses. Section 2.2 addresses the various insurance and insurance-like instruments that investors can rely upon to hedge against default risk; these include sovereign

[1] This chapter intentionally disregards three basic aspects of sovereign lending: the interest rate, the maturity, and the amount loaned (the riskier the country, the higher its interest rate, the shorter its debt maturity, and the smaller the amount issued). These features are analyzed in Chap. 4.

N. Gaillard, *When Sovereigns Go Bankrupt*, SpringerBriefs in Economics,
DOI 10.1007/978-3-319-08988-1_2

risk insurance covenants, contracts of guarantee offered by multilateral agencies, and credit default swaps (CDSs).

2.1 Protection Clauses in Bond and Loan Covenants

2.1.1 The Long Road to Enforcement of Sovereign Debt Contracts

State sovereign immunity has long been a barrier for creditors that wanted to recover unpaid amounts. In the nineteenth century, sovereign borrowers were not liable to being sued in any foreign court unless they had expressly submitted to this forum. Furthermore, the position of borrowers even in their own tribunals was contingent upon constitutional rules. In *Twycross v. Dreyfus* (1877), George Jessel – then Master of the Rolls – stated that:

> [Sovereign bonds] amount to nothing more than engagements of honour, binding, so far as engagements of honour can bind, the government which issues them, but are not contracts enforceable before the ordinary tribunal of the country which issued them without the consent of the government of that country.

As a result, bondholders essentially had only two avenues for retrieving their money: convincing their government to employ gunboat diplomacy or seeking some arrangement with the defaulting country.[2] This explains why arbitration clauses were often added to foreign government debt contracts (Waibel 2011, pp. 158–160; Weidemaier 2010, pp. 342–344). In fact, arbitration became a conventional means of settling debt disputes at the turn of the twentieth century. The Permanent Court of Arbitration (PCA) was established in 1899 at the first Hague Peace Conference to provide services for the arbitration and resolution of debt disputes. The PCA's decisions, although morally reinforced after the Drago–Porter Convention of 1907, did not yet have any binding force. This shortcoming was overcome in 1922 when the Permanent Court of International Justice (PCIJ) was established under the auspices of the League of Nations.[3] In the famous *Serbian loans* and *Brazilian loans* cases (1929), the PCIJ provided details about the law that presumably was to govern sovereign debt contracts. It stated that "any contract which is not a contract between states in their capacity as subjects of international law is based on the municipal law of some country" (i.e., the domestic law of a sovereign state; Schmitthoff 1937, p. 185).

---

[2] These two approaches were not entirely exclusive. Prior to their military intervention in Venezuela in 1902, Great Britain, Germany, and Italy had proposed to submit their dispute to a neutral tribunal (Fischer Williams 1925, pp. 311–312).

[3] Article 59 of the statute for the PCIJ was provided for by article 14 of the covenant of the League of Nations.

The absence of international law to resolve disputes between private creditors and sovereign debtors seemingly foreshadowed the decline of arbitration clauses, which increasingly became regarded as a lack of commitment from borrowers (Waibel 2011, p. 167). Instead, from the 1940s onward, investors sought legal enforcement by pushing for governing law clauses, provisions that subjected sovereign issuers to being sued in foreign courts, and/or covenants that included a waiver of immunity from suit or execution (Choi et al. 2012, pp. 138–140).

Along these lines private creditors obtained support from US authorities. In 1952, the US Department of State issued the Tate Letter; this document allowed for sovereign immunity for public acts only, thus excluding commercial acts.[4] Although the policy prescribed thereby could not prevent a sovereign bond issuer from asserting its immunity ex ante or from obtaining the withdrawal of its waiver (if any) from the US Department or a court, it was a milestone in the restrictive theory of sovereign immunity (Weidemaier 2014, pp. 77–79). That policy became codified with the enactment in 1976 of the Foreign Sovereign Immunities Act (FSIA), which established that immunity determinations were contingent upon courts and not on the US Department of State. Perhaps more importantly, the statute affirmed that waivers of sovereign immunity from suit and execution were henceforth binding and irrevocable. Even if a foreign government had not waived its immunity, its property was not immune from execution provided it was "used for the commercial activity upon which the claim [was] based." The enactment of the FSIA led to a complete re-drafting of sovereign bond covenants. Despite being almost nonexistent until then, waivers of immunity from suit were frequently included clauses starting in the late 1970s (Weidemaier 2014, p. 88).[5] A further step was taken with the US Supreme Court's explicit statement that the issuance of debt was a commercial act (*Republic of Argentina v. Weltover*, 1992). Thereafter, waivers of immunity were retained in foreign government debt contracts – probably because such contracts contained provisions for adjudication in both American and foreign courts and provided details regarding service of process (Delaume 1994, pp. 267–268).

While the restrictive theory of sovereign immunity gained ground in Western countries, creditors endeavored to impose new enforcement terms that sometimes were complementary to waivers of immunity. For instance, "consent to jurisdiction" clauses and governing law clauses – which stipulate that sovereign borrowers subject themselves to the jurisdiction of a foreign country and to a foreign law, respectively – were systematically included in sovereign bond contracts after the outbreak of the Latin American debt crisis in 1982 (Choi et al. 2012, pp. 154–158).

---

[4] That distinction accorded with Grotius' analysis, which opposed acts of the state *qua* sovereign and acts of the state *qua* private person.

[5] During the years that followed, other countries passed similar laws – for example, United Kingdom and Canada in 1978 and 1982, respectively (Brownlie 2003, p. 326). France, Germany, and Switzerland had revised the principle of absolute immunity as early as the nineteenth century (Delaume 1957, pp. 203–204). These shifts support the view that *creditor* nations have long promoted a restrictive theory of sovereign immunity.

Scrutinizing governing law clauses, Das et al. (2012, p. 41) find that, as of March 2009, 69 % and 22 % of outstanding emerging market bonds issued in international markets were governed by (respectively) New York law and London law. Because the chosen law matches the selected jurisdiction, it reveals that the American and British legal systems have become central to resolving sovereign debt disputes.[6]

Since the 1970s, restriction of sovereign immunity for debt covenants has been of considerable help to creditors seeking to enforce their contract terms. However, creditors may be deprived of their rights if they attempt to seize a defaulted borrower's assets, particularly when those assets are located in a territory over which the foreign court has no jurisdiction or when the decision rendered by the foreign court is less favorable to bondholders than expected.[7] In the nineteenth century and the interwar years, the prospect of such impediments to their claims convinced some creditors to demand security interests from borrowers.

2.1.2 *Securing Debt*

In terms of security clauses, two broad categories of debt must be distinguished: general obligation bonds and secured bonds.

General obligation bonds are backed by the full faith, credit, and taxing powers of the issuer. This means that the sovereign borrower is obliged to raise all revenues available to honor its financial commitments. For Borchard (1951, pp. 82–83), such clauses are redundant because "they merely confirm in emphatic terms a fact resulting by implication from the obligation."

In contrast, the repayment of *secured bonds* depends on specific collateral: revenue streams or assets. Secured bonds are generally issued to protect against the discontinuity of debt reimbursement. It is therefore not surprising that the revenues or the assets earmarked are contingent upon the economic profile of the debtor country. In 1922, for example, Brazil issued a 7.5 % external bond worth £9 million that was secured by a mortgage on about 4,535,000 bags of coffee, which represented the government's entire stock and was valued at more than £13 million (*Moody's Manual* 1922, p. 32). More frequently, low- and middle-income countries were constrained to pledge customs duties in order to borrow (e.g., Ecuador, Uruguay, and Nicaragua; CFB 1895, pp. 109–110, 347; *Moody's Manual* 1929, p. 791); however, various revenues and taxes could be used to reach this objective (revenues from railway, water works, port facilities, tobacco, etc.).[8] In some cases,

[6] The hegemony of New York was driven in part by the enactment in 1984 of "Section 5-1401 of New York's General Obligations Law, which validates stipulations of New York law without a requirement of a reasonable connection between the transaction and New York" (Committee on Foreign and Comparative Law 2013, pp. 5–6).

[7] In the *NML v. Argentina* decisions (28 March 2013), the French Supreme Court tightened the conditions applied to waivers of sovereign immunity from execution.

[8] Borchard (1951, pp. 83–91) provides many examples of security clauses.

bondholders exercised direct administration of pledged revenues through agents, ad hoc organizations, or monopolies received from the debtor country. Such methods of enforcement were sometimes implemented by creditor nations (e.g., France, Germany, Great Britain, and the United States) on behalf of bondholders (Borchard 1951, pp. 91–93; Waibel 2011, pp. 42–57).

It is worth emphasizing that lenders claimed inordinate levels of securitization for countries that had recently defaulted. The Mexican and Venezuelan debt issuances of 1888 and 1905, respectively, reflect this uncompromising approach. The Mexican government had to offer as security "20 % of the net export and import duties and the total net proceeds of the direct taxes on land, houses, industries, etc." The security required of Venezuela was "60 % of the ordinary customs duties of [its] ports, with the exception of La Guayra and Puerto Cabello." These customs duties had to be paid "separately by the merchants, and placed at the Banco de Venezuela to a separate account" (CFB 1904, p. 261; CFB 1907, pp. 431–432).

Yet unless the debtor country was under the political and administrative supervision of a great power, collateral security turned out to be of little help to foreign investors when the borrower was unwilling to repay its debt or faced a collapse of its economy. So ever since the second part of the twentieth century, other types of clauses have been preferred by creditors (see Appendix 2 for some specific clauses added to a sovereign bond contract).

2.1.3 Avoiding Subordination

Instead of securing their bonds or loans, lenders have sought to prevent sovereign borrowers from creating liens over their assets or revenues in favor of other creditors – that is, without securing the current debt on an equal basis. Such "negative pledge" clauses were part of the World Bank's and multilateral development banks' loan contracts in the late 1940s. For policy reasons, these institutions were reluctant to demand collateral security but could not accept that future lenders would benefit from doing so (Buchheit and Pam 2004, pp. 899–900). Private bankers followed suit in the 1970s after Citigroup, a creditor of Zaire, managed to prevent two competitor firms from granting a secured loan to Zaire by successfully arguing that Citigroup's contract included provisions comparable to a negative pledge (Buchheit and Pam 2004, pp. 902, 909; *Wall Street Journal*, "Citibank Sues over Repayment of Debt by Zaire," 10 August 1976). Subsequently, negative pledge became a boilerplate clause in unsecured bonds and notes prospectuses issued by speculative-grade (i.e., risky) countries (e.g., Arab Republic of Egypt 2007, p. 73; Republic of El Salvador 2011, p. 64; Republic of Ghana 2007, p. 68; Republic of Paraguay 2013, p. 110; Republic of the Philippines 2003, p. 111; Ukraine 2012, p. 20).

Pari passu clauses are another type of provision included in bonds and loans to preclude discrimination among creditors. In the nineteenth century, such clauses were often used in secured debt instruments because different lenders had frequently been offered the same collateral. In the aftermath of World War II, the decline of secured debt issuances was accompanied by the insertion of negative pledge clauses conjoined with pari passu provisions (Buchheit and Pam 2004, pp. 894–906). The use of freestanding pari passu clauses spread in the 1980s to protect creditors against involuntary subordination resulting from local law procedures. Today, however, there are two interpretations of these provisions. Buchheit and Pam (2004, pp. 917–918) state the narrow interpretation: pari passu clauses mean only that a debt ranks equally in right of payment with all other unsubordinated debts. Cohen (2011, pp. 14–17) presents a broader interpretation. Endorsing the decision of the Brussels Court of Appeal in *Elliott Associates, L.P. v. Banco de la Nacion* (2000), Cohen affirms that pari passu clauses oblige a defaulted sovereign to "pay similarly situated creditors equally, at the same time and to the same extent, in all payment situations." This controversy bears watching because it could have a significant impact on sovereign debt restructuring processes.

2.1.4 Avoiding Monetary Erosion

Ensuring the legal enforcement and the securing of their claims (while avoiding subordination) are necessary but not sufficient conditions for creditors to derive their expected returns. Among other parameters, creditors must therefore carefully examine the currency in which their bonds are denominated. This explains why creditors have traditionally preferred to lend in their own currency – or in an international currency – to protect against monetary erosion. This preference is the contrapuntal aspect of the "international original sin" problem highlighted by Eichengreen et al. (2005a, pp. 13–14).[9]

Even though it prevents monetary erosion, lending funds to a sovereign in other than its domestic currency is not a panacea: countries that suffer from original sin are also vulnerable to exchange rate volatility; this is likely to exacerbate the currency mismatch and lead to reversals in capital inflows, thus jeopardizing the debtor's creditworthiness.[10] In their study of foreign currency borrowing during the nineteenth and twentieth centuries, Bordo et al. (2010, pp. 648–649) find that higher ratios of foreign currency debt to total debt are related to increased risks of currency crises and defaults. Creditors are therefore on the horns of a dilemma when

[9] Recall that "international original sin" refers to the inability to borrow abroad in domestic currency. This problem affects not only developing and emerging countries with a poor track record and high inflation but also small economies that, despite their fiscal and monetary credibility, have only an embryonic financial system (Eichengreen et al. 2005b, pp. 234–238).

[10] This reasoning applies also to foreign currency-indexed debt and to bonds or loans that incorporate gold clauses (in the nineteenth century and during the interwar years) or foreign exchange clauses.

choosing the currency denomination of a foreign government bond. A possible compromise is to opt for inflation-indexed bonds. Finland is reported to have introduced this type of debt instruments as early as 1945. Israel, Iceland, Brazil, Chile, Colombia, Argentina, Great Britain, Australia, Mexico, Canada, Sweden, and New Zealand did likewise during the following decades (Campbell and Shiller 1996, pp. 156–158; Henry Gemmill, "Fancy Finance: 'Inflation-Proof' Bonds Are the Rage in Israel, Finland, France, Austria," *Wall Street Journal*, 9 February 1956).

2.1.5 Arranging for Guaranteed Debt

Investors naturally favor guaranteed debt, especially when the guarantee is issued by another sovereign or a pool of sovereigns whose creditworthiness is considered substantially stronger (i.e., creditor nations that themselves borrow at lower interest rates or have higher credit ratings). Such clauses provide that the "guarantor undertakes to be answerable for the payment of the debt in case the principal debtor should fail to perform his engagement" (Borchard 1951, p. 105). A guarantee clause may be added to loan or bond covenants for economic or diplomatic reasons.

In 1855, in the midst of the Crimean War, the Ottoman Empire issued a 4 % note whose interest payments were guaranteed by its two allies: Great Britain and France. In 1923, Austria managed to re-access capital markets thanks to a League of Nations loan whose interest and principal were guaranteed by Belgium, Czechoslovakia, Denmark, France, Great Britain, Italy, the Netherlands, and Sweden (Decorzant and Flores 2012, p. 13). The repayment of these two loans was not subsequently discontinued, in contrast to the fate of other contemporaneous Ottoman and Austrian securities.

More recently, Egypt issued in 2005 a 10-year, US dollar-denominated note fully guaranteed – with respect to both principal and interest – by the US government acting through the United States Agency for International Development (Arab Republic of Egypt 2007, pp. 18, 67). Similarly, in 2012, the United States affirmed its strong commitment to the democratic transition in Tunisia by signing a sovereign loan guarantee agreement with the Tunisian government.[11]

The World Bank has also implemented credit guarantee schemes available to all countries eligible for borrowing from the International Bank for Reconstruction and Development (IBRD) or the International Development Association (IDA) (Independent Evaluation Group 2009, pp. 10–13). For example, policy-based guarantees (PBGs) and partial credit guarantees (PCGs) support government borrowing from commercial lenders or government bond issues; PBGs are offered for general balance of payments support, and PCGs are offered for projects approved by the World Bank.

[11] http://www.state.gov/s/d/met/releases/198355.htm

2.1.6 *Facilitating Debt Restructurings*

Debt renegotiation clauses have three idiosyncratic features. First, they are not designed to enforce contract terms but rather to minimize creditors' losses – in the event of default – by making debt restructurings easier. Indeed, the 1930s showed that stubborn opposition to any sovereign debt restructuring scheme could be counterproductive and costly to lenders (Adamson 2002, pp. 498–499).

Second, they illustrate the prioritization of bondholders' collective rights over individual rights when a loan is restructured. The resulting collective action clauses may take various forms.[12] The most prominent CACs are collective *modification* clauses, which enable a qualified majority of bondholders to make decisions that become binding on all holders (typically a debt restructuring), and collective *acceleration* clauses, which limit the ability of holdout bondholders to prevent a restructuring.

The third distinguishing feature of renegotiation clauses is that, although sovereign debt contracts included CACs as far back as the early 1900s (Weidemaier and Gulati 2012, pp. 16–22), they were seldom used before 2003.[13] Collective action clauses were praised by the US Treasury Department as a means of addressing the moral hazard problem (Gelpern and Gulati 2006, pp. 1653–1654). However, the IMF (2002, pp. 27–28) expressed a more skeptical view; as its then First Deputy Managing Director, Anne Krueger, advocated instead a quasi-statutory approach via implementation of a sovereign debt restructuring mechanism.

2.2 Hedging and Insurance Contracts

When purchasing sovereign debt, creditors may individually sign distinct contracts to protect against default. Two types of instruments merit further discussion.

2.2.1 *Hedging Instruments*

Bondholders have long sought to hedge against adverse price movements and defaults. In 1824, Rothschild had lent funds to Naples and then sold part of the underwritten bonds to the public. However, the financial difficulties experienced by Latin American countries at the time[14] were a widespread concern among investors,

[12] See Choi et al. 2012 (pp. 159–166) for an overview of the different CACs.

[13] The issuance by Mexico of bonds with both types of CACs in February 2003 served as a catalyst for the inclusion of collective modification and collective acceleration clauses in most debt covenants.

[14] Chile and Colombia defaulted in 1826 and Mexico in 1827 (CFB 1878, pp. 52–53).

who feared that Naples might become insolvent. Rothschild therefore proposed in 1827 the purchase of future coupons of Neapolitan bonds in order to support prices (Gille 1965, p. 168). Although primarily intended to preserve Rothschild's own reputation, this proposal was a seminal opportunity for bondholders to insure against sovereign default. Yet it remained an exceptional form of hedging because creditors generally preferred inserting provisions into debt covenants (see Sect. 2.1).

It was not until 1991 that similar instruments – namely, the credit default swaps (CDSs) – were introduced on a much larger scale in the corporate debt market and later in the sovereign debt market (Rancière 2002, p. 15; Smithson and Mengle 2006, p. 54).[15] The International Swaps and Derivatives Association (ISDA), a global trade association representing participants in the Over-the-Counter (OTC) derivatives industry, provides the following definition of the CDS: it is "a contract designed to transfer the credit exposure of debt obligation between parties. The buyer of a credit swap receives credit protection, whereas the seller of the swap guarantees the creditworthiness of the underlying security. In a CDS the risk of default is transferred from the holder of the security to the seller of the swap." The CDS *spread* is the annual amount the CDS buyer must pay the seller over the length of the contract. Expressed in basis points, it is a percentage of the notional amount (1 basis point = 0.01 %)

The CDS is triggered when the reference entity (i.e., the debt issuer) experiences a credit event on an obligation. A credit event is "an event linked to the deteriorating creditworthiness of an underlying reference entity in a credit derivative. The occurrence of a credit event usually triggers full or partial termination of the transaction and a payment from protection seller to protection buyer." For a sovereign CDS (SCDS), credit events include failure to pay, restructuring, obligation acceleration, obligation default, and debt moratorium or repudiation.

Outstanding SCDS notional amounts reached USD2.941 trillion by the end of 2012 (BIS 2013, p. 20). The top-ten CDS reference entities were Italy, Spain, France, Brazil, Germany, Turkey, Mexico, Russia, South Korea, and Japan; together these countries accounted for 55 % of all SCDSs (IMF 2013a, p. 60).

2.2.2 *Guarantee Insurance Contracts*

Export credit agencies (e.g., the US Export-Import Bank, Coface, and Euler-Hermes) have traditionally secured foreign direct investment flows to emerging and developing countries by mitigating certain types of risk. These risks include

[15] Credit default swaps are not equivalent to insurance contracts for two main reasons. First, the "buyer does not have to own the underlying security, or otherwise have any insurable interest in that security"; second, "the buyer does not in fact have to suffer any loss in order to recover on the CDS" (Garbowski 2008, p. 4). An examination of the use of CDS instruments for speculating or basis trading purposes is beyond the scope of this book.

currency inconvertibility and transfer restrictions; expropriation without due compensation; war, terrorism, and civil disturbance; breach of contract; and failure to honor financial obligations. In particular, the Export-Import Bank provides guarantees that cover loans granted by US investors to sovereign governments.

In response to the development of sovereign bond markets since the 1990s, insurance companies have entered this market. Established in 1997, Sovereign Risk Insurance Ltd. offers loan guarantees to cover financial losses due to nonpayment of amounts owed by governments. This firm paid several claims to European banks following defaults by the Dominican Republic and the Seychelles in 2005 and 2009, respectively.[16] The American International Group, Inc. (AIG 2006, pp. 5–9) provides insurance against failures of a government to honor (i) its payment obligations under a promissory note, bond, sovereign loan, or sovereign guarantee; (ii) its hard currency or local currency payment obligations under a guarantee agreement issued in support of a project; or (iii) its payment obligations under a purchase contract, irrespective of whether such payment obligations are denominated in hard currency or local currency. Zurich Insurance Group (Zurich 2009, p. 1) offers insurance against a sovereign not honoring its own guarantee; this insurance covers financial institutions in the event of payment defaults by a government.

International organizations have followed suit. In 2009, the Multilateral Investment Guarantee Agency (MIGA) launched its Non-Honoring of Sovereign Financial Obligations (NHSFO) coverage to protect lenders against losses resulting from a sovereign default. This guarantee is available to investors only if the payment obligation of the debtor government is unconditional and not subject to any defenses. In 2012, MIGA provided Société Générale with a NHSFO guarantee to cover a loan to the government of Ghana (MIGA 2012, pp. 20–21).[17]

[16] http://www.sovereignbermuda.com/claims_history/claims_history.html

[17] This loan was made to finance the completion of a power plant.

Chapter 3
Preventing Sovereign Defaults

Abstract Chapter 3 investigates how some investors have been able to interfere with the debtor's economic policy by insisting that measures be taken to reduce the risk of default in the short and medium term. Such interference can be direct or may be more subtle. Section 3.1 analyzes the role played by certain financial and economic advisors to foreign governments, many of whom were affiliated with a public or private institution that was a creditor to the focal country. Section 3.2 addresses the concept of conditionality and shows how states, bankers, and such international institutions as the International Monetary Fund (IMF) have made their lending conditional on the implementation of specific policies. There is a specific focus on the conditionality imposed by the International Monetary Fund. The IMF's policy instruments have traditionally involved currency devaluation to boost exports, anti-inflationary measures to restore monetary credibility, and fiscal restraint to reduce public indebtedness.

Keywords Economic advising • Money doctor • Conditional lending • Conditionality • IMF • Adjustment program

In addition to insurance instruments and contractual protection clauses, some investors have been able to interfere with the debtor's economic policy – insisting that measures be taken to reduce the risk of default in the short and medium terms. Such interference may be direct or more subtle. Section 3.1 analyzes the role played by certain financial and economic advisors to foreign governments. Section 3.2 focuses on the concept on conditionality and shows how creditors – states, bankers, and such international institutions as the IMF – have made their lending conditional on the implementation of specific policies.

3.1 Financial and Economic Advising

Foreign governments and central banks have long hired consultants and advisors in order to benefit from their expertise. As early as the 1850s, Jean-Gustave Courcelle-Seneuil, a French economist, was invited by the Chilean government to redraft banking laws (Glaser 2003, pp. 167–168). Much more recently, Jeffrey Sachs has

N. Gaillard, *When Sovereigns Go Bankrupt*, SpringerBriefs in Economics,
DOI 10.1007/978-3-319-08988-1_3

served as special advisor to various emerging and developing countries.[1] Are such experts – sometimes called "money doctors" because their policy recommendations included currency stabilization and reform of the central bank – independent? Some economists seem to have used their advisory role to promote their own economic agendas but it is hard to believe that their advice was either disinterested or entirely disconnected from any political or financial lobbying – despite hints to contrary given by Edwin Kemmerer (1927, p. 2), a professor at Princeton University and economic advisor to Latin American and European governments. There are many examples of economic advisors to a foreign government who were affiliated with a public or private institution that was a creditor to that country. Three cases are examined here.

From 1924 to 1929, Kemmerer worked not only for several foreign governments but also for Dillon, Read & Co. This US investment bank was the lead underwriter of the sovereign bonds issued by Poland and Bolivia, two countries for which Kemmerer was then serving as a consultant (Rosenberg and Rosenberg 1987, p. 77).[2] The objective of Dillon, Read & Co. was obviously to exploit Kemmerer's reputation. The bank lent money to governments that were on the verge of enhancing their macroeconomic fundamentals in response to Kemmerer's recommendations and hence of being perceived as less risky by market participants.

A few years later, another money doctor – Otto Niemeyer, advisor to the Bank of England – was invited by Brazil and Argentina to reshape their respective central banks (Abreu and de Souza 2011, pp. 18–21). Niemeyer was clearly serving as the eyes of British bondholders, who did their best to prevent the default of these Latin American economies. Yet, in the midst of the Great Depression, this type of mission fell short of convincing governments to continue paying their debts. That is why Great Britain took what was then the drastic step of signing trade agreements. For instance, the 1933 Roca-Runciman Treaty stipulated that Great Britain would import some of Argentina's cereal and meat production in exchange for the preservation of British investors' interests in Buenos Aires.

A third illustration of the tight relationships between creditors and financial advisors is the Bloomfield mission in South Korea. Following World War II, the United States sought to stimulate the economic recovery of several European and Asian countries. Toward that end, the Economic Cooperation Act of 1948 created the Economic Cooperation Administration; its purpose was to furnish material and financial assistance to many nations, including South Korea. The next year, Arthur Bloomfield – economist at the Federal Reserve Bank of New York – was sent to Seoul with the aim of redrafting the charter of Korea's central bank and launching monetary reforms to fight inflation (Alacevich and Asso 2009, pp. 261–265). This financial advisory mission was intended not only to save the South Korean economy but also, and more fundamentally, to anchor that country in the Western camp.

[1] http://jeffsachs.org/about

[2] Naturally, this conflict of interest was not disclosed at the time.

3.2 Conditional Lending

Investors have at their disposal even more direct and intrusive methods for ensuring that debtors will respect their financial obligations. Namely, investors may impose certain conditions – which are quite different in nature from the protection clauses inserted into bond and loan covenants – on the availability of funds. Such stipulations are encapsulated in the notion of "conditionality". Although this notion is closely connected in the economic literature to IMF behavior since the 1950s (Polak 1991, p. 1), conditionality was evident prior to the birth of the Bretton Woods Agreement. For the purposes of this discussion, lending will be viewed as *conditional* when it is contingent on the direct or indirect, ex ante or ex post interference, supervision, or control of the means or goals of the borrower's economic, trade, monetary, banking, and/or fiscal policy with the aim of ensuring that the borrowing country will repay its debt.[3] Conditionality has been employed by creditor states (Sect. 3.2.1), banks (Sect. 3.2.2), and the IMF (Sect. 3.2.3).[4]

3.2.1 Conditionality Imposed by Creditor States

Until the early twentieth century, European powers did not hesitate to use gunboat diplomacy as a means of forcing a country to honor its financial commitments (Mitchener and Weidenmier 2005, p. 35). However, such military interventions were not so common and were abandoned after the Drago–Porter Convention of 1907. Instead, creditor governments interfered in the economic policies of debtor sovereigns in order to protect themselves against the "bankruptcy" of those countries.

Following its default in 1894 and its unsuccessful war against Turkey 3 years later, Greece was granted in 1898 a 2.5 % loan guaranteed by France, Great Britain, and Russia. At the same time an international financial commission was established in Athens. As legal representative of foreign bondholders in Greece, this commission oversaw the revenues assigned to service the country's public debt and supervised the administrations responsible for producing those revenues (Borchard 1951, pp. 291–292).

The United States acted similarly when laying the foundations of its "dollar diplomacy" at the turn of the twentieth century. In 1907, a $20 million loan was offered by Kuhn, Loeb – a prestigious US investment house – to the Dominican Republic. This loan was conditioned upon the ratification of a treaty between Washington and Santo Domingo: that treaty vested control of the Dominican public debt in the President of the United States and provided for the appointment of a

[3] In this chapter, I address only *macroeconomic* conditionality.

[4] See Koeberle et al. (2005) for a review of conditionality as imposed by the World Bank.

general receiver of Dominican customs, who was to collect all duties (Rosenberg 1999, pp. 42–47).

In 1928, the French government set four conditions on a loan to its Romanian counterpart: (i) Bucharest promised not to approach the League of Nations about stabilizing its currency, the leu; (ii) the loan would be funded jointly by French and US capital; (iii) Romania accepted the necessity of reaching an agreement to fund its outstanding debt to France; and (iv) one sixth of the loan would be earmarked for the purchase of French products (*Moody's Manual* 1929, p. 841; Moreau 1954, pp. 432, 516). The last provision runs counter to the definition of conditionality used in this chapter because it focuses on microeconomic issues. Provisions of this type flourished in the protectionist context of the 1930s.

The advent of the IMF and the World Bank in 1944 institutionalized the notion of multilateralism, which made it more difficult for creditor countries to interfere directly in the fiscal or monetary policy of a debtor government. Although bilateral loans continue to be made – in particular, through such development finance institutions as the United States Agency for International Development and the French Development Agency – the approach is now radically different. These agencies conduct microeconomic analyses before lending funds to finance basic services: water infrastructures, electricity, agriculture, and healthcare. In addition to their funding instruments (concessional and nonconcessional loans, grants, etc.), such agencies offer technical engineering and support to recipient countries. Chinese bilateral lending, which is likewise not predicated on macroeconomic conditionality, nonetheless relies on two fundamental conditions: adherence to its so-called one-China policy and the use of Chinese contractors, technologies, and workers (Mattlin and Nojonen 2011, pp. 16–20).

3.2.2 *Conditionality Imposed by Banks*

Financial institutions have historically possessed few means for persuading a sovereign not to default. Unlike creditor countries, they cannot engage in either military or retaliatory trade measures. Furthermore competition between investors precludes banks from exerting direct control over a sovereign borrower's fiscal or debt policy. However, there was a noteworthy exception to such powerlessness.

The tight relationships between Brazil and Rothschilds from the 1850s to the 1920s[5] enabled the investment bank to influence and even, on one occasion, to dictate Brazilian economic policy (Shaw 2005, pp. 171–183). During the period 1896–1898, which saw a precipitous decline in coffee prices, Brazilian public debt soared and a debt restructuring appeared to be imminent. Rothschilds agreed to grant a £8.6 million funding loan provided that the Brazilian government implemented a deflationary monetary policy and an orthodox fiscal policy based

[5] At the time, Rothschilds underwrote most of the Brazilian government bonds.

on increasing domestic taxes and reducing government expenditures (Fishlow 1989, pp. 92–93).[6] Not surprisingly, this stringent conditionality was driven by the strong desire of Rothschilds to preserve its reputation as the world's leading investment bank.

Since the Rothschilds era, bankers have seldom attempted to direct a sovereign's public finances. Consider the case of Citibank, which lent funds to Peru in 1976 while planning to oversee that country's economic policy (Lipson 1981, pp. 622–623). This strategy was an utter failure, lending credence to the view that conditionality had become an exclusive prerogative of international institutions like the IMF.

3.2.3 *Conditionality Imposed by the IMF*

International Monetary Fund conditionality can be traced in part to the first League of Nations loans of the early 1920s.

An embryonic form of conditionality was set up in 1922 when the League loan offered to Austria was made contingent on (i) the appointment of a commissioner-general tasked with the responsibility of monitoring whether the Austrian government implemented fiscal measures adequate to balance its budget and (ii) the establishment of a control committee to protect the interests of nations that guaranteed the loan (Borchard 1951, pp. 296–299; Schuker 2003, p. 58). That funds were contingent on macroeconomic adjustments was sometimes perceived as undermining the borrower's sovereignty. For instance, Portugal refused a League-sponsored loan in 1927 on the grounds that the international organization's requirements were politically unacceptable (Wynne 1951, pp. 384–385). The Great Depression and the resurgence of nationalism signalled the demise of the League of Nations. With the establishment of the IMF and its expanding role starting in the 1980s, the concept of conditionality began to predominate; it also became controversial in emerging and developing economies.

Conditionality as imposed by the IMF has evolved significantly since the first financial support packages were negotiated in the 1950s. At least four reasons can be advanced to explain this evolution: the occurrence of dissimilar economic and financial crises, the changing profile of countries that have sought credit, the shift in some economic paradigms, and experience gained over the years. All these factors affected the objectives of IMF lending policies as well as the means for reaching them.[7]

Programs supported by the IMF (e.g., the stand-by arrangements launched in 1952) were initially designed to solve balance-of-payments difficulties in both

[6] This austerity plan depressed economic activity and contributed to the banking crisis of 1900.

[7] The terms "lending policy", "adjustment program", "stabilization program", and "structural program" are used interchangeably hereafter.

developing and developed countries. In fact, the Fund staff was asked early on to take measures to correct an increasing number of imbalances.[8] This goal boosted the IMF's activity and led to a more formal and sophisticated conditionality framework (see Table 3.1 for a description of the main programs sponsored by the IMF).

The cornerstone of conditionality is the *letter of intent* (see Appendix 3A for an example), which describes the loan's purpose and the economic and financial policies that the borrower has committed to implementing. Next, compliance with IMF requirements is checked via program reviews that assess the fulfillment of performance criteria and the achievement of indicative targets (IMF 2014, pp. 1–2; Polak 1991, pp. 12–16). Disbursements under an IMF program depend on the approval or completion of reviews by the IMF Executive Board. For the most part, performance criteria and targets are quantitative; they may include a ceiling on new external loans contracted by the government, a minimum level of international reserves, and/or a specific timetable for fiscal deficit reduction (see Appendix 3B for a case study). Yet qualitative criteria are also employed. For example, the adjustment program for South Korea in December 1997 mandated the closure of nonviable commercial banks, the temporary nationalization of other banks, the strengthening of bank supervision, and improvements in the corporate governance system (Neiss et al. 2009, pp. 24–26).

The IMF's policy instruments have traditionally involved currency devaluation to boost exports, anti-inflationary measures to restore monetary credibility, and fiscal restraint to reduce public indebtedness.[9] Since the 1990s, the "Washington consensus" has led the IMF to promote market-based policies and to emphasize competitiveness (Guitian 1995, p. 812); another consequence is a broadening and refinement of conditionality practices. For instance, the IMF has developed bilateral and multilateral surveillance capacities to monitor (respectively) the economic policies of member countries and global trends in the world economy. Bilateral country surveillance relies on meetings between a team of IMF economists and the focal sovereign; those meetings serve as a basis for country reports. Multilateral surveillance is conducted by way of macroeconomic analyses, which are published in the *World Economic Outlook*, the *Global Financial Stability Report*, and the *Fiscal Monitor*. Meanwhile adjustment programs have involved technical assistance on monetary, fiscal, and statistical issues.

The IMF structural programs have been regularly denounced for several decades. Jeffrey Sachs (1989) and Joseph Stiglitz (2002) argue that they lead to contractionary policies, depressed economic growth, and a weakening of the poor. Such criticism was recently vindicated by the IMF's mea culpa: the Fund admitted

[8] "An imbalance arises whenever the sum total of demands for resources in an economy exceeds the amount of those resources that can be generated internally plus those that can be attracted from abroad on an appropriate scale and on sustainable terms" (Guitian 1995, p. 798).

[9] These conclusions are drawn from a comparison of several IMF stabilization programs during the past five decades; see Johnson and Salop (1980) and Brau and McDonald (2009).

Table 3.1 IMF Financing Facilities

	Credit facility (year adopted)	Purpose	Conditions	Phasing and monitoring	Schedule (years)
Credit tranches and extended fund facility	Stand-By Arrangement (SBA) (1952)	Medium-term assistance for countries with balance-of-payments difficulties of a short-term character	Adopt policies that provide confidence that the member's balance-of-payments difficulties will be resolved within a reasonable period	Quarterly purchases (disbursements) contingent on observance of performance criteria and other conditions	3.25–5
	Extended Fund Facility (EFF) (1974) (Extended Arrangement)	Longer-term assistance to support members' structural reforms to address balance-of-payments difficulties of a long-term character	Adopt up to 4-year program with structural agenda and with annual detailed statement of policies for the next 12 months	Quarterly or semiannual purchases (disbursements) contingent on observance of performance criteria and other conditions	4.5–10
	Flexible Credit Line (FCL) (2009)	Flexible instrument in the credit tranches to address all balance-of-payments needs, potential or actual	Very strong ex ante macroeconomic fundamentals, economic policy framework, and policy track record	Approved access available up front throughout the arrangement period, subject to a midterm review after 1 year	3.25–5
	Precautionary and Liquidity Line (PLL) (2011)	Instrument for countries with sound economic fundamentals and policies	Strong policy frameworks, external position, and market access, including financial sector soundness	Large front-loaded access subject to semiannual reviews (for 1- to 2-year PLL)	3.25–5
Special facilities	Rapid Financing Instrument (RFI) (2011)	Rapid financial assistance to member countries facing an urgent balance-of-payments need	Efforts to solve balance-of-payments difficulties (may include prior actions)	Outright purchases without the need for full-fledged program or reviews	3.25–5

(continued)

Table 3.1 (continued)

	Credit facility (year adopted)	Purpose	Conditions	Phasing and monitoring	Schedule (years)
Facilities for low-income members under the poverty reduction and growth trust	Extended Credit Facility (ECF) (2010)	Medium-term assistance to address protracted balance-of-payments problems	Adopt 3- to 4-year ECF arrangements; ECF programs are based on Poverty Reduction Strategy Papers prepared by countries in a participatory process and on integrating macroeconomic, structural, and poverty reduction policies	Semiannual (or sometimes quarterly) disbursements contingent on observance of performance criteria and reviews	5.5–10
	Standby Credit Facility (SCF) (2010)	To resolve short-term balance-of-payments and precautionary needs	Adopt 12- to 24-month SCF arrangements	Semiannual disbursements contingent on observance of performance criteria and reviews	4–8
	Rapid Credit Facility (RCF) (2010)	Rapid assistance for urgent balance-of-payments needs when an upper-credit-tranche-quality program is not needed or feasible	No review-based program necessary or ex post conditionality	Usually in a single disbursement	5.5–10

Source: IMF (2013c, pp. 38–39)

that fiscal consolidation had been associated with lower growth than expected, which suggests that its lending policy had been inadequate in some cases (Blanchard and Leigh 2013, pp. 19–20). This controversy should remind economists that preventing a sovereign default may entail high political and social costs.[10]

[10] Another group of critics have alleged that moral hazard problems are inherent to IMF-supported programs. Addressing such criticism is beyond the scope of this book.

Chapter 4
Anticipating Sovereign Debt Crises

Abstract Chapter 4 studies the various tools that investors can use to discriminate among borrowers and forecast debt crises. Section 4.1 describes the traditional indicators of sovereign risk – bond yields and spreads as well as ratings provided by Fitch, Moody's, Standard & Poor's (S&P), and Euromoney Country Risk (ECR) – and identifies their determinants. It is worth noting that sovereign bond spreads reflect more than country-specific fundamentals; in contrast to other risk indicators, risk premiums are strongly affected by liquidity and market sentiment. Section 4.2 compares these various indicators. Credit rating agencies and ECR ratings are strongly correlated with one another, but their correlation with 1- and 10-year sovereign bond yields is relatively weak. Section 4.3 demonstrates that sovereign debtors must overcome seven types of risk in order to preserve their creditworthiness: natural disaster, geopolitical risk, institutional and political risk, economic risk, monetary and exchange rate risk, fiscal and tax-system risk, and debt-related risk.

Keywords Spread • Yield • Sovereign rating • Rating agency • Sovereign risk • Debt sustainability

This chapter focuses on the various tools that investors can use to discriminate among borrowers and forecast debt crises. Section 4.1 describes the traditional indicators of sovereign risk – from market yields to credit ratings – and identifies their determinants. Section 4.2 compares these various indicators. Section 4.3 demonstrates that sovereign debtors must overcome seven types of risk in order to preserve their creditworthiness.

4.1 Traditional Indicators of Sovereign Risk

Since the nineteenth century, investors have used several different indicators of sovereign risk. Until 1914, the creditworthiness of a country was strongly correlated with the size and reputation of the bank that underwrote its bonds (Flandreau et al. 2010, pp. 61–66). Not surprisingly, new sovereign risk indicators were proposed during and/or immediately after debt crises. Sovereign ratings were first

N. Gaillard, *When Sovereigns Go Bankrupt*, SpringerBriefs in Economics,
DOI 10.1007/978-3-319-08988-1_4

issued in 1918 following the massive debt accumulated by WWI belligerents (Gaillard 2011, p. 4). Credit ratings by Institutional Investor, International Country Risk Guide (ICRG) and Euromoney Country Risk (ECR) were launched in 1979, 1980, and 1982 (respectively), a period during which the growing debt of developing countries was a major concern among American and European bankers (Sachs 1986, pp. 402–403). The volume of sovereign credit default swaps (SCDSs) increased dramatically in the 1998–1999 aftermath of the Asian crisis and Russia's default (Packer and Suthiphongchai 2003, p. 81). That being said, sovereign interest rates on the primary and secondary markets remain the oldest and the most basic indicators.

4.1.1 Interest Rate Spreads

Interest is charged by lenders to borrowers as compensation for the transfer of a certain amount of funds. At least theoretically, if all else is held equal then a larger loan amount and a longer debt maturity both translate into a higher interest rate (or, in the case of bonds, a higher coupon rate).[1] However, many other criteria affect interest rates. The most prominent factors are the borrower's default risk, the monetary policy of major economic powers, the availability of liquidity in capital markets, and the risk of financial contagion. This is why investors track interest rate spreads – that is, differences between the yield on risk-free bonds and yields on sovereign bonds of specific countries.

Because a greater interest rate spread reflects a higher default risk as perceived by market participants, it is crucial to assess exactly what underlies. Consider the major lending booms since the nineteenth century. During the last three decades of the *Pax Britannica*, the main determinants of sovereign spreads were default history and the ratio of debt service to revenues (Flandreau and Zumer 2004, pp. 38–39). Another important factor was commitment to gold convertibility, which reduced the yield on a country's bonds by some 40 basis points (Bordo and Rockoff 1996, pp. 408–413). In the 1920s, high debt ratios remained strongly correlated with high borrowing costs; however, default history was no longer as significant (Obstfeld and Taylor 2003, pp. 260–265). The determinants of the spreads during the commercial bank lending boom that occurred in the second half of the 1970s did not differ radically from what they had been a century earlier. The ratios of debt to gross national product (GNP), reserves to GNP, and public investment to GNP were key variables used by lenders to discriminate among debtor nations (Edwards 1984, pp. 730–732). The first two of these, in addition to the economic growth rate and

[1] This relation does not always hold empirically. First of all, large bond issues tend to be more liquid and so their spreads are more likely to decline over time. Second, inversions of the term structure of interest rates (i.e., long-term rates being lower than short-term rates) are not uncommon; in fact, they often predict a recession (see Harvey 1993, p. 6).

ratio of exports to GDP, were the main economic determinants of the spreads between emerging market sovereign bonds and US Treasury bonds during the period 1998–2002 (Rowland and Torres 2004, pp. 34–37). Yet as increasing numbers of lower-middle-income countries managed to access financial markets in the 2000s, fiscal and political factors became major criteria in setting sovereign risk premiums (Baldacci et al. 2008, pp. 13–15).

Although creditors have for 150 years relied on the same indicators to determine sovereign bond spreads, such spreads are likely to fluctuate substantially over time and possibly within a short period – even for countries that have *not* experienced significant change in their political, financial, or macroeconomic fundamentals. There are various reasons for such volatility, which is not directly related to default risk as that term is normally understood.

The financial re-globalization of the 1990s has increased the mobility of capital and made the strategies of portfolio investors more sensitive to events, extraneous to the sovereign debtor, that could alter the risk-return trade-off.

A shift in US monetary policy exemplifies such an event. From 1994 through 1999, US 10-year Treasury yields had a direct and positive effect on the bond spreads of emerging countries (Arora and Cerisola 2001, pp. 479–488). Even more interesting is that not only the level but also the volatility of other US interest rate benchmarks (e.g., the 3-month Fed funds futures rates) were key determinants of the boom and bust of sovereign bond spreads during 1991–2007 (Hartelius et al. 2008, pp. 15–17). That higher uncertainty about the expected stance of US monetary policy contributes to widening risk premiums was recently illustrated in a new manner. In May 2013, the Federal Reserve's announcement that it might taper its purchases of US securities in the short term led to a decline in exchange rates and a consequent rise in the sovereign bond spreads of major emerging markets (Eichengreen and Gupta 2013, pp. 4–7).

The US monetary policy is but one of the factors that affect capital inflows to emerging and developing countries. For instance, a decline in risk aversion (as proxied by the Chicago Board Options Exchange Volatility Index, VIX),[2] accounted for more than 40 % of the compression of emerging spreads recorded between December 2002 and February 2007 (Hartelius et al. 2008, p. 20). Investor appetite for risk has traditionally been an opportunity for countries with a high ex ante default risk to access capital and obtain better borrowing conditions than would otherwise be justified by their fundamentals.[3] Conversely, confidence crises are likely to trigger a scarcity in the availability of international capital. Beyond systemic risk events that may jeopardize the viability of economic and financial institutions (e.g., the 2008 collapse of Lehman Brothers), the Barings debacle of

[2] This index is a measure of the market's expectations of near-term volatility as reflected by S&P 500 stock index option prices.

[3] During the 1920s, the search for high yields by market participants led to a deterioration in the quality of sovereign bonds issued on the New York Stock Exchange (NYSE); see Mintz (1951, pp. 29–40).

1890 and the Mexican peso crisis of 1994 have shown that a single country's severe financial problems can affect other sovereign borrowers (Mitchener and Weidenmier 2007, pp. 17–32; Kaminsky et al. 2003, pp. 55–58). It is worth noting that such financial contagion effects are stronger today than in the late nineteenth century (Mauro et al. 2002, pp. 714–721).

Finally, sovereign bond spreads reflect more than country-specific fundamentals. Liquidity and market sentiment also play a key role in determining risk premiums, in contrast to other risk indicators as sovereign ratings.

4.1.2 Sovereign Ratings

Sovereign ratings first appeared in 1918 in *Moody's Analyses of Investments – Government and Municipal Securities*. At the time, only ten foreign countries were rated: Argentina, Canada, Cuba, the Dominican Republic, France, Japan, Norway, Panama, Switzerland, and the United Kingdom (Gaillard 2011, p. 4). By the mid-1920s, Moody's expanded its coverage to include all sovereign bond issuers while three competitor rating agencies emerged: Poor's, Standard Statistics, and Fitch.[4] Sovereign rating activity declined in the aftermath of the Great Depression and remained moribund for nearly four decades – because foreign governments had no recourse to capital markets for raising funds. However, sovereign bond markets were reinvigorated by the growth in borrowing needs of both developed and industrialized countries and by the establishment of market-based macroeconomic policies from the 1980s (Williamson 1990). These developments spurred the resumption of sovereign ratings: Standard & Poor's rated 13 countries in 1983, 37 in 1993, 93 in 2003, and 128 in 2013.

The significance of a sovereign credit rating has not changed since the interwar years: it consists of an opinion regarding the relative ability and willingness of a government to meet its financial commitments. Today, CRAs assign long-term and short-term credit ratings in both foreign currency (FC) and local currency (LC). Table 4.1 presents Fitch, Moody's, and Standard & Poor's long-term rating scales.

There are three reasons for the success of CRAs. First, the growth of bond markets in the 1920s and from the 1980s onward has legitimated the role of credit risk analysts and thereby boosted the profits of Fitch, Moody's, and Standard & Poor's. Second, the extensive use of credit ratings among bankers and investors enabled CRAs to gain credibility. Since the 1920s, an ever-increasing number of market participants have set internal rules based on credit ratings (Robinson 1929, pp. 557–558). Examples of credit ratings embedded in investment rules include setting minimum rating requirements for bond purchases, maximum portfolio shares by rating category, maximum single-security exposure by rating category, retention guidelines for downgraded securities that no longer meet eligibility

---

[4] Poor's and Standard Statistics merged in 1941 to form Standard & Poor's.

Table 4.1 Current meanings of ratings issued by the big three CRAs

Category	Fitch ratings	Moody's ratings	S&P ratings	Significance
Investment grade	AAA	Aaa	AAA	Lowest credit risk
	AA+	Aa1	AA+	Very low credit risk
	AA	Aa2	AA	
	AA–	Aa3	AA–	
	A+	A1	A+	Low credit risk
	A	A2	A	
	A–	A3	A–	
	BBB+	Baa1	BBB+	Moderate credit risk
	BBB	Baa2	BBB	
	BBB–	Baa3	BBB–	
Speculative grade	BB+	Ba1	BB+	Substantial credit risk
	BB	Ba2	BB	
	BB–	Ba3	BB–	
	B+	B1	B+	High credit risk
	B	B2	B	
	B–	B3	B–	
	CCC+	Caa1	CCC+	Very high credit risk
	CCC	Caa2	CCC	
	CCC–	Caa3	CCC–	
	CC		CC	
	C			
Default	RD	Ca	SD	RD and SD designate issuers that have defaulted on part of their debt; Ca designates defaulting issuers for which there is some prospect of recovering the principal and interest
	D	C	D	D designates issuers that have defaulted on all of their debt; C designates defaulting issuers for which there is little prospect of recovering the principal or interest

Sources: Author's classification based on fitchratings.com, moodys.com, and standardandpoors.com

guidelines, and performance benchmarking relative to ratings-based bond indices; moreover, ratings typically underpin discussions between fund managers and clients (Cantor et al. 2007, pp. 13–26). Third, the insertion of credit ratings into regulatory rules – a practice that began in the early 1930s – installed CRAs as the gatekeepers to financial markets. Regulations have increasingly relied on credit ratings since the re-globalization of the 1980s.[5]

[5] Only recently have US and European legislators decided to counter overreliance on CRAs by removing references to credit ratings in regulations; as evidenced by the Dodd-Frank Wall Street Reform and Consumer Protection Act of July 2010 and by Regulation (EU) No. 462/2013 of the

Such dependence on the opinions of Fitch, Moody's, and Standard & Poor's explains why changes in sovereign rating affect risk premiums. For example, downgrades widened emerging countries' spreads during the period 1987–2007. This effect was even more significant when a country's rating was lowered from investment-grade to speculative-grade status (Cantor and Packer 1996, pp. 47–48; Gaillard 2011, pp. 164–169). In contrast, market participants seek to anticipate – rather than react to – upgrades (Reisen and von Maltzan 1999, pp. 11–14).

It is more instructive to examine the determinants of sovereign ratings. The ratings assigned by Fitch, Moody's, and Standard & Poor's have been a function of the same macroeconomic and institutional variables since the interwar years: the ratio of GDP per capita and of FC debt to exports (or revenues), inflation, default history, and institutional stability (Gaillard 2011, pp. 50–60). Credit rating agencies also take remittance flows into account when rating small, low- and middle-income countries (Avendaño et al. 2011, pp. 63–68).

Nonetheless, CRAs have failed to anticipate debt crises; for instance, Venezuela was rated triple-A when it defaulted in 1983. More recently, Greece and Cyprus were still ranked in the single-A and double-A categories 2 years prior to their respective debt restructurings in 2012 and 2013. Those excessively high ratings obliged CRAs to announce substantial downgrades. In 1932, Fitch and Moody's downgraded more than 80 % of the sovereign bonds listed on the NYSE (Flandreau et al. 2011, p. 516). The eurozone turmoil was a similarly painful episode: within a span of 2 years, Moody's lowered its ratings of Greece's and Cyprus' credit by 15 notches.[6] The inability of Fitch, Moody's, and Standard & Poor's to forecast these latter two defaults compromised their rating accuracy (Gaillard 2014a, pp. 217–220; Gaillard 2014b, pp. 131–136) and thus induced them to amend their methodologies.

In fact, the CRAs' sovereign ratings criteria were not only updated but also made more transparent. Regulation (EU) No. 462/2013 of the European Parliament and of the Council of 21 May 2013 amending Regulation (EC) No. 1060/2009 on credit rating agencies requires CRAs to provide a "detailed evaluation of the changes to the quantitative assumption justifying the reasons for the rating change and their relative weight". Standard & Poor's (2013) and Moody's (2013b) complied with this new European rule by publishing enhanced methodologies.

Consider the methodology now employed by Moody's. It focuses on four broad rating factors: a country's economic, institutional, and fiscal strengths as well as its susceptibility to event risk. Each of these factors consists of several subfactors. Economic strength (Factor 1) is based on growth dynamics, scale of the economy, and national income, which account for (respectively) 50 %, 25 %, and 25 % of the Factor 1 score. Growth dynamics include three variables: average real GDP growth, volatility in real GDP growth, and the World Economic Forum global

European Parliament and of the Council of 21 May 2013 amending Regulation (EC) No. 1060/2009 on credit rating agencies.

[6] The two reference periods are December 2009-July 2011 and February 2011-January 2013.

competitiveness index. Scale of the economy and national income refer to the size of the nominal GDP and the GDP per capita, respectively. Moody's usually incorporates two adjustment factors into its assessment of economic strength: diversification of the country's economy and the risk of a credit boom. After estimating or calculating each subfactor, the outcomes for each indicator are mapped to one of 15 ranking categories that range from very high plus (VH+) to very low minus (VL–). These mappings are used to determine the score for the subfactors and also for the broader rating factors. Next, Factors 1 and 2 (economic and institutional strengths) are combined with equal weight to yield the economic resiliency factor. The combination of this new factor with Factor 3 (fiscal strength) yields an assessment of the government's financial strength, which is finally combined with Factor 4 (susceptibility to event risk) to obtain an indicative credit rating.

A ratings methodology of this type is relatively transparent and hence much more in line (than were traditional CRA practices) with other sovereign risk indicators.

4.1.3 Euromoney Country Risk Ratings

Institutional Investor, ICRG, and ECR emerged in the early 1980s – a time when CRAs issued very few sovereign ratings. This section examines ECR ratings, which are widely used by investors (see e.g. Citi 2013, pp. 7–12).

The ECR methodology involves a set of quantitative and qualitative criteria derived from survey responses of nearly 400 economists and financial analysts. The resulting factors are classified into six broad categories: economic risk (30 % weighting), political risk (30 %), structural risk (10 %), access to capital markets (10 %), debt indicators (10 %), and sovereign ratings (10 %).

The economic risk category comprises the following elements: stability of the banking system, GNP outlook, unemployment, government finances, and monetary policy. The political risk category includes corruption, risk of non-repatriation, government stability, access and transparency of information, institutional risk, and the regulatory and policy environment. Assessment of structural risk is based on an analysis of demographics, hard and soft infrastructures, and labor market relations. Access to capital markets depends mainly on interest rates. For lower-income countries, debt indicators are calculated using the ratios of debt service to exports, total debt stocks to GNP, and current account balance to GNP; for higher-income countries, only the last two ratios are used. Finally, sovereign ratings are those issued by Fitch, Moody's, and Standard & Poor's. The assessments of these various factors are then converted into a single score by means of a standardized scoring chart. The final ECR rating can range from 100 (ideal, risk-free country) to 0.[7]

[7] The ratings issued by Euromoney are unsolicited, unlike most of the ratings assigned by CRAs.

Table 4.2 Correlations among sovereign risk indicators, 14 January 2014

	Fitch ratings	Moody's ratings	S&P ratings	ECR ratings
Fitch ratings	1 (106)	N.R.	N.R.	N.R.
Moody's ratings	0.956 (96)	1 (126)	N.R.	N.R.
S&P ratings	0.974 (99)	0.960 (114)	1 (129)	N.R.
ECR ratings	0.906 (102)	0.888 (121)	0.896 (118)	1 (186)
1-year bond yield	0.551 (45)	0.544 (47)	0.558 (46)	0.506 (47)
10-year bond yield	0.607 (53)	0.572 (55)	0.623 (55)	0.586 (55)

Sources: Author's computations based on data from fitchratings.com, moodys.com, standardandpoors.com, euromoneycountryrisk.com, and investing.com

Notes: The table reports R-squared values, with the number of pairwise observations given in parentheses. "N.R." = not relevant

4.2 Comparison of Sovereign Risk Indicators

The ratings issued by Fitch, Moody's, Standard & Poor's, and ECR are strongly correlated with one another, but their correlation with 1- and 10-year sovereign bond yields is weaker (see Table 4.2 for the correlations and Appendix 4 for the data). There are several reasons for this discrepancy.

First, as an endogenous indicator of risk, a bond yield reflects a country's cost of financing whereas an external rating measures the likelihood of a default. Second, CRAs' ratings – and, to a lesser extent, ECR ratings – assess only credit risk. In addition to credit risk, bond yields (and spreads) reflect other types of risks (e.g., liquidity and currency risks), which increases their volatility; see Sect. 4.1.1. Third, ECR and CRAs (especially Moody's) employ "through-the-cycle" rating methodologies. Such methods do not account for cyclical and temporary components of default risk (Löffler 2004, pp. 695–720), which explains why their ratings are updated on an annual basis (quarterly for ECR).[8] In contrast, bond yields are momentary risk measurements that fluctuate from day to day. The result is a weaker correlation between sovereign spreads and ratings in times of very high and very low risk aversion (Gaillard 2011, pp. 153–158) as well as a delayed reaction of CRAs to any significant and persistent increase in bond yields or SCDSs (Gaillard 2014a, pp. 220–223).

4.3 Threats to Sovereign Creditworthiness

History has shown that CRAs and also investors often fail to anticipate debt crises. This failure is due largely to the various causes of sovereign default and to the suddenness with which a country's credit position can weaken. Seven major threats

[8] Starting on 1 January 2014, CRAs are required to revise their ratings of European Union countries three times a year in accordance with Regulation (EU) No. 462/2013 of the European Parliament and of the Council of 21 May 2013.

may be identified: natural disaster, geopolitical risk, institutional and political risk, economic risk, monetary and exchange rate risk, fiscal and tax-system risk, and debt-related risk. These threats are next discussed in turn.

4.3.1 *Natural Disaster*

Volcanic eruptions, floods, droughts, cyclones, earthquakes, and tsunamis are adverse events that may oblige low- or middle-income countries to restructure their public debt. Following the 1999 Izmit earthquake, Turkey imposed a retroactive withholding tax on interest income from all outstanding domestic currency securities issued by the government prior to December 1999; Moody's considers such action a default (Moody's 2013a, p. 22). In 2010, 6 months after the earthquake that hit Haiti, the IMF approved full cancellation of the country's outstanding liabilities to the Fund and approved an Extended Credit Facility Arrangement to support reconstruction (IMF 2010). A devastating natural disaster is difficult to factor into credit ratings and bond yields because its probability is extremely low. However, when one occurs it is likely to trigger a default and lead to heavy financial losses.

4.3.2 *Geopolitical Risk*

Geopolitical risk can take different forms. A belligerent government may deliberately default or declare a debt moratorium to fund its war, especially when fighting against its creditors (e.g., Italy and Japan in 1940 and 1942, respectively). A country may also miss a payment or be forced to reschedule its debt following an invasion (e.g., Kuwait and Czechoslovakia in 1990 and 1938–1946). And any country subject to frequent cross-border terrorist attacks will find it difficult to access capital markets or get low borrowing costs (e.g., Lebanon during the recent decades).[9] More generally, even the prospect of war – or of destabilizing military or paramilitary action – has a negative effect on sovereign risk indicators. The reluctance of Moody's to give high ratings to Gulf states, for instance, follows from the "regional geopolitical vulnerabilities" of those countries (Moody's 2007, p. 1).

[9] About 10 % of a Lebanon's bond prospectus is devoted to the geopolitical and political situation (Lebanese Republic 2009, pp. 15–28).

4.3.3 Institutional and Political Risk

The quality and the resilience of a country's institutional and political regime have several components: the extent to which citizens view those institutions as being legitimate, the effectiveness of the rule of law, the coherence of the electoral system, and the ability of major political parties to agree on main economic issues.

The defaults of Russia in 1918 and of Cuba in 1960 are both closely related to coups that occurred a few months earlier. Until then, these countries were ruled by market-friendly dictatorships that were threatened by far-leftist but popular terrorist organizations. Yet recent history shows that weak democratic governments (e.g., Latin American countries since the 1980s) can also fall into "bankruptcy". In order to measure the robustness of institutional and political regimes in 200 countries, Kaufmann et al. (2010) developed a system of Worldwide Governance Indicators. These researchers constructed aggregate indicators of six broad dimensions of governance: voice and accountability, political stability and absence of violence, government effectiveness, regulatory quality, rule of law, and control of corruption. Not surprisingly, the average scores of these six indicators are highly correlated with credit ratings.[10]

4.3.4 Economic Risk

The economic prosperity of a country is fundamentally linked to how well its firms specialize in profitable market segments, implement innovative strategies, export to fast-growing areas, and keep labor costs under control. A good proxy for a country's economic strength is its overall competitiveness.

Once each year, the World Economic Forum (WEF) publishes its "Global Competitiveness Report". For the WEF, the 12 main determinants of competitiveness are institutions, infrastructure, macroeconomic stability, health and primary education, higher education and training, goods market efficiency, labor market efficiency, financial market sophistication, technological readiness, market size, business sophistication, and innovation (WEF 2009, pp. 4–7). A sharp drop in a country's ranking on this scale may signal a serious inadequacy in its economic landscape and a potential weakening of its credit position in the medium term. Greece is an edifying illustration: it was ranked 37th in 2004 but slipped to the 71st position in September 2009 (WEF 2004, p. xiii; WEF 2009, p. 13)[11] – that is,

[10] A comparison of the 2012 average scores to the ECR ratings as of 14 January 2014 yields an R-squared value exceeding 0.6 (author's computations based on www.govindicators.org and www.euromoneycountryrisk.com).

[11] Nine countries ranked ahead of Greece in 2009 were not included in the 2004 report: Azerbaijan, Barbados, Brunei, Kazakhstan, Kuwait, Oman, Puerto Rico, Qatar, and Saudi Arabia. Thus, Greece's relative ranking has fallen at least 25 places in 5 years.

2 months before the Greek government announced that the budget deficit would be more than double the previous forecast and 30 months prior to its debt restructuring.

4.3.5 Monetary and Exchange Rate Risk

Sovereign debt issuers face three challenges in terms of monetary and exchange rate policy. First, they must curb inflation. This objective has been met by most countries: in 2012, only 12 % of them had a double-digit inflation rate.[12] Second, they must overcome the "international original sin" problem; otherwise, a country will find it necessary to borrow in a foreign currency. In such cases the sovereign is then obliged to restrain its public indebtedness (and limit the depreciation of its domestic currency) or else run the risk of becoming insolvent (Eichengreen et al. 2005a, pp. 20–31). Third, the government and its central bank must monitor the sustainability of their exchange rate vis-à-vis major currencies. The defaults of Argentina in 2001 and of Greece in 2012 were driven in part by high appreciation of the peso and euro (respectively), which undermined the competitiveness of those countries. This issue is still a hot topic in the eurozone because the "pain threshold" – beyond which the EUR/USD exchange rate appreciation significantly impairs economic recovery – is lower for France (1.24) and Italy (1.17) than the exchange rate (1.38) prevailing as this book is written (i.e., April 2014) (Deutsche Bank 2013, pp. 3–8).

4.3.6 Fiscal and Tax-System Risk

A fundamental objective for both high- and middle-income countries should be to implement growth-oriented tax reforms. Such reforms involve increasing taxes on immovable property, reducing the corporate income tax, broadening the personal income tax and value-added taxes, and minimizing administrative, enforcement, and compliance costs (OECD 2010, pp. 83–99).

However, an efficient tax policy must be combined with a sustainable fiscal policy. A government that cannot reach a primary or even a fiscal surplus in times of high GDP growth (e.g., Argentina in 1996–1998, Greece in 2003–2007) will be vulnerable in the event of an economic slowdown. Southern European countries with costly welfare-state systems can learn from Scandinavian economies that managed to preserve their model by recalibrating their social policies (Hemerijck 2013, pp. 152–220).

[12] Author's computations based on the World Bank's World Development Indicators.

4.3.7 Debt-Related Risk

A key component of economic policy is to ensure that public and private debts are sustainable in the short and medium terms.

The sustainability of *public* debt involves several factors. First, a country needs to diversify its funding sources and to manage debt efficiently if illiquidity is to be avoided (Dornbusch and Draghi 1990, pp. 1–13). Toward that end, gold and foreign exchange reserves should be accumulated if possible. Second, the growth of central government debt cannot be persistently higher than GDP growth. Third, the ultimate use of new debt should be carefully appraised: will it finance productive investments or merely an increase in civil servant jobs? Finally, in light of the greater responsibilities devolving to subnational entities, it has become indispensable to monitor local debt issuers (Canuto and Liu 2013, pp. 1–30).[13]

The recent banking crises in Iceland, Ireland, and Spain demonstrate that regulators and central bankers must pay increasing attention to the growth of *private* debt. Housing bubbles are especially pernicious because they artificially boost GDP growth before bursting and triggering a recession (Reinhart and Rogoff 2009, pp. 158–162). Also, since a government may be compelled to bail out a distressed bank that is "too big to fail", it is crucial to supervise and scrutinize the activities of systemic financial intermediaries. Any prolonged surge in the ratio of average domestic private-sector credit to GDP (or of bank assets to GDP) is cause for alarm because it indicates an increased risk of future contingent liabilities for the central government.

[13] From this viewpoint, the Brazilian Fiscal Responsibility Law of 2000 – which set limitations on personnel expenditures and ceilings for public-sector debt for the federal government as well as for states and municipalities – was a milestone in the restoration of the country's credit position.

Conclusion

This book has explained how and why the relation between creditors and sovereign debtors has evolved since the 1820s. Although it has become increasingly difficult for foreign governments to renege on their financial commitments, "sovereign bankruptcies" are still frequent: no fewer than 94 countries defaulted on their FC debt in the twentieth century. As a result, investors and bankers have been obliged to develop various tools to anticipate and protect against such threats. Experience suggests that investors' monitoring should rely on credit ratings in times of low risk aversion but shift to bond yields if an economic slowdown has been ascertained and risk aversion is climbing (Gaillard 2014b, pp. 129–131).

When the borrowing costs of a debt-burdened government become excessively high (e.g., Greece starting in January 2010), it is sometimes too late to implement austerity programs. Since the turn of the twenty-first century, such policies have failed to restore sovereign creditworthiness and have actually amplified debt crises in two major cases: Argentina in 2000–2002 and Greece in 2010–2012. These failures support two views. On the one hand, there is an idiosyncratic debt threshold beyond which a particular country is especially vulnerable in cases of adverse economic, financial, or political events (Reinhart et al. 2003); exceeding that threshold will likely lead to a restructuring of that country's debt. On the other hand, fiscal consolidation measures may simply be too late and inefficient to compensate for previous unsound macroeconomic policies and past fiscal profligacy (IMF 2013b).

For that reason, some governments have tried to overcome the "default or consolidate" dilemma by exerting *financial repression* (Reinhart 2012). This approach – which may include (among other measures) negative interest rates, purchases of sovereign debt by the central bank, capital controls, a tax policy that constrains savers to buy and hold sovereign bonds, and/or stricter supervision and control of the banking sector – has been used by the governments of both industrialized and developing countries. The financial repression phenomenon trims creditors' returns and reflects the ongoing complex relations among a state, its central bank, and its creditors. More fundamentally, it shows that any government is

N. Gaillard, *When Sovereigns Go Bankrupt*, SpringerBriefs in Economics,
DOI 10.1007/978-3-319-08988-1

capable of taking heterodox monetary or financial measures to remain solvent. In other words, a struggling sovereign borrower is a unique debtor because it may adopt the path of least resistance and continue to honor its financial obligations.

Appendix 1A: Sovereign Debt Restructurings, 1970–2010

Date	Country	Debt affected (USD mil.)	Date	Country	Debt affected (USD mil.)
Sept. 1978	Jamaica	63	Oct. 1988	Malawi	35
April 1979	Jamaica	149	Nov. 1988	Brazil	62,100
June 1979	Turkey	429	June 1989	Zaire	61
Aug. 1979	Turkey	2,269	June 1989	Nigeria	5,829
Jan. 1980	Peru	340	July 1989	Poland	206
April 1980	Zaire	402	Oct. 1989	Honduras	132
Dec. 1980	Nicaragua	582	Oct. 1989	South Africa	7,500
June 1981	Jamaica	89	Dec. 1989	Trinidad & T.	446
Aug. 1981	Turkey	100	Feb. 1990	Mexico	54,300
Nov. 1981	Madagascar	147	Feb. 1990	Philippines	2,120
Dec. 1981	Nicaragua	192	April 1990	Madagascar	49
Mar. 1982	Nicaragua	100	May 1990	Costa Rica	1,384
Mar. 1982	Turkey	2,269	June 1990	Jamaica	332
April 1982	Poland	1,957	Sept. 1990	Morocco	3,200
Nov. 1982	Poland	2,225	Sept. 1990	Senegal	37
Dec. 1982	Liberia	30	Dec. 1990	Chile	6,494
Dec. 1982	Romania	1,598	Dec. 1990	Venezuela	19,585
Jan. 1983	Zaire	58	Jan. 1991	Uruguay	1,610
Feb. 1983	Brazil	4,452	Mar. 1991	Niger	111
Mar. 1983	Malawi	57	Dec. 1991	Mozambique	124
June 1983	Romania	567	Dec. 1991	Nigeria	5,883
July 1983	Nigeria	1,350	Mar. 1992	Algeria	1,457
July 1983	Peru	380	Nov. 1992	Brazil	9,167
July 1983	Uruguay	575	Nov. 1992	Guyana	93
Aug. 1983	Mexico	18,800	Dec. 1992	Philippines	4,471
Sept. 1983	Costa Rica	609	Feb. 1993	Uganda	153
Sept. 1983	Nigeria	585	April 1993	Argentina	28,476

(continued)

N. Gaillard, *When Sovereigns Go Bankrupt*, SpringerBriefs in Economics,
DOI 10.1007/978-3-319-08938-1

Date	Country	Debt affected (USD mil.)	Date	Country	Debt affected (USD mil.)
Sept. 1983	Yugoslavia	950	April 1993	Bolivia	171
Oct. 1983	Ecuador	970	July 1993	Paraguay	20
Nov. 1983	Chile	2,169	Sept. 1993	South Africa	5,000
Nov. 1983	Poland	1,192	Dec. 1993	Jordan	1,289
Dec. 1983	Cuba	130	April 1994	Brazil	43,257
Jan. 1984	Brazil	4,846	May 1994	Gabon	187
Jan. 1984	Chile	1,160	June 1994	Bulgaria	7,910
Feb. 1984	Nicaragua	145	June 1994	Zambia	570
Feb. 1984	Senegal	77	Aug. 1994	Dom. Rep.	1,087
Mar. 1984	Niger	27	Aug. 1994	Panama	452
April 1984	Nigeria	925	Aug. 1994	Sao Tome & P.	10
May 1984	Yugoslavia	1,250	Oct. 1994	Poland	13,531
June 1984	Zaire	64	Feb. 1995	Ecuador	7,170
June 1984	Jamaica	165	June 1995	Slovenia	812
July 1984	Poland	1,390	Aug. 1995	Albania	501
Aug. 1984	Ecuador	350	Aug. 1995	Sierra Leone	235
Oct. 1984	Madagascar	195	Nov. 1995	Nicaragua	1,100
Dec. 1984	Cuba	103	Jan. 1996	Ethiopia	226
Mar. 1985	Mexico	28,600	May 1996	Panama	3,936
May 1985	Zaire	61	July 1996	Algeria	3,200
May 1985	Costa Rica	440	July 1996	Croatia	858
May 1985	Senegal	20	Aug. 1996	Mauritania	53
July 1985	Cuba	90	Dec. 1996	Senegal	80
Aug. 1985	Argentina	9,900	Mar. 1997	Macedonia	229
Aug. 1985	Mexico	20,100	Mar. 1997	Peru	10,600
Sept. 1985	Jamaica	369	Dec. 1997	Bosnia & Herz.	1,300
Oct. 1985	Panama	579	Dec. 1997	Russia	30,500
Oct. 1985	Sudan	920	Dec. 1997	Togo	75
Dec. 1985	Ecuador	4,224	Dec. 1997	Vietnam	782
Dec. 1985	Yugoslavia	3,600	Mar. 1998	Cote d'Ivoire	6,462
Feb. 1986	Dom. Rep.	823	June 1998	Kenya	91
Feb. 1986	Morocco	538	Sept. 1998	Ukraine	420
Feb. 1986	Venezuela	20,307	Oct. 1998	Ukraine	109
April 1986	Chile	6,007	Dec. 1998	Guinea	130
April 1986	Niger	52	Mar. 1999	Russia	4,933
April 1986	Philippines	3,242	July 1999	Pakistan	777
May 1986	Zaire	65	Aug. 1999	Ukraine	163
July 1986	Uruguay	1,958	Dec. 1999	Guyana	56
Sept. 1986	Brazil	6,671	Dec. 1999	Pakistan	610
Sept. 1986	Poland	1,970	Feb. 2000	Russia	1,307
Sept. 1986	Romania	800	April 2000	Ukraine	1,598
Mar. 1987	Mexico	52,300	Aug. 2000	Ecuador	6,700
Mar. 1987	South Africa	10,900	Aug. 2000	Russia	31,943

(continued)

Date	Country	Debt affected (USD mil.)	Date	Country	Debt affected (USD mil.)
May 1987	Zaire	61	Feb. 2001	Yemen	607
May 1987	Jamaica	285	Aug. 2001	Honduras	13
May 1987	Mozambique	253	May 2002	Cameroon	600
June 1987	Chile	5,901	Oct. 2002	Moldova	40
June 1987	Madagascar	60	May 2003	Uruguay	3,127
Aug. 1987	Argentina	29,515	Aug. 2003	Cameroon	796
Sept. 1987	Morocco	2,444	Jan. 2004	Tanzania	156
Nov. 1987	Nigeria	4,249	April 2004	Moldova	115
Dec. 1987	Gabon	39	July 2004	Serbia & Mont.	2,700
Dec. 1987	Philippines	9,690	Sept. 2004	Dominica	144
Jan. 1988	Nigeria	1,213	April 2005	Argentina	60,572
Feb. 1988	Gambia	19	May 2005	Dom. Rep.	1,100
Mar. 1988	Bolivia	473	Oct. 2005	Dom. Rep.	180
Mar. 1988	Mexico	3,671	Nov. 2005	Grenada	210
Mar. 1988	Uruguay	1,770	Jan. 2006	Iraq	17,710
April 1988	Guinea	43	Feb. 2007	Belize	516
May 1988	Togo	49	Dec. 2007	Congo	2,100
July 1988	Poland	8,441	June 2009	Ecuador	3,190
Sept. 1988	Yugoslavia	6,895	Feb. 2010	Seychelles	320
Sept. 1988	Venezuela	20,338	April 2010	Cote d'Ivoire	2,940

Source: Cruces and Trebesch's (2011) database
Notes: This table includes medium- and long-term debt restructurings with foreign private creditors. It excludes debt restructurings that predominantly affected domestic creditors and official creditors

Appendix 1B: Foreign Debt Adjustment Plan of 1943 Affecting Brazilian External Debt

Brazilian Decree-Law no. 6019 of 23 November 1943 fixed definitive norms for the payment and service of external loans granted by public issuers and denominated in either GBP or USD. Article 1 stipulated that, effective 1 January 1944, the payment of interest and amortization of the bonds of external loans issued in pounds sterling or dollars by federal, state and municipal governments, by the Coffee Institute of the State of Sao Paulo, and by the Banco do Estado de Sao Paulo would be made in accordance with either "Plan A" or "Plan B" – at the option of the bondholders. Plan A maintained the original face value of the bond while establishing new rates of interest and quotas for amortization. Under Plan B, the bond's original face value was reduced but investors were compensated by cash payments along with revised interest rates and amortization quotas.

	Plan A		Plan B			
	Rates (in %)		Rates (in %)			
	Interest	Amort.	Paid in cash	Principal reduced to	Interest	Amort.
Loans issued in USD						
Funding, 1931, 5 %	3.375	1.53	12.5	80	3.75	2.65
Guaranteed, 1921, 8 %	3.500	1.59	15.0	80	3.75	2.65
Guaranteed, 1922, 7 %	3.500	1.59	15.0	80	3.75	2.65
Guaranteed, 1926, 6.5 %	3.375	1.54	12.5	80	3.75	2.65
Guaranteed, 1927, 6.5 %	3.375	1.54	12.5	80	3.75	2.65
Coffee Realization, 1930, 7 %	3.500	1.59	15.0	80	3.75	2.65
Loans issued in GBP						
Funding, 1898, 5 %	3.375	3.08	12.5	80	3.75	4.63
Funding, 1914, 5 %	3.375	0.98	12.5	80	3.75	1.48
Funding, 1931, 20 years, 5 %	3.375	5.74	12.5	80	3.75	8.61
Funding, 1931, 40 years, 5 %	3.375	1.47	12.5	80	3.75	2.20
Guaranteed, 1903, 5 %	2.750	0.80	5.0	80	3.75	1.30
Guaranteed, 1927, 6.5 %	3.375	0.37	12.5	80	3.75	0.61

(continued)

N. Gaillard, *When Sovereigns Go Bankrupt*, SpringerBriefs in Economics,
DOI 10.1007/978-3-319-08988-1

	Plan A		Plan B			
	Rates (in %)		Rates (in %)			
	Interest	Amort.	Paid in cash	Principal reduced to	Interest	Amort.
Not guaranteed, 1883, 4.5 %	1.625	1.88	9.0	50	3.75	6.10
Not guaranteed, 1888, 4.5 %	1.625	1.44	9.0	50	3.75	4.68
Not guaranteed, 1889, 4 %	1.500	0.40	7.5	50	3.75	1.30
Not guaranteed, 1895, 5 %	1.750	0.50	10.5	50	3.75	1.62
Not guaranteed, 1901, 4 %	1.500	1.04	7.5	50	3.75	3.36
Not guaranteed, 1910, 4 %	1.500	0.36	7.5	50	3.75	1.16
Lloyd, 1910, 4 %	1.500	10.56	7.5	50	3.75	34.22
Port Works, 1911, 4 %	1.500	2.18	7.5	50	3.75	7.06
Ceara Railway, 1911, 4 %	1.500	0.34	7.5	50	3.75	1.10
Port Works, 1913, 5 %	1.750	0.42	10.5	50	3.75	1.36
Coffee Realization, 1930, 7 %	3.500	9.16	15.0	80	3.75	13.74

Source: FBPC (1945, pp. 143–146)
Note: This table includes only sovereign and quasi-sovereign bonds

Appendix 2: Contractual Clauses Included in the "$546,786,000 – U.S. Dollar Bonds Due 2029" Issued by Belize in 2007

New Issue: Eligible Claims were entitled to be exchanged for the New Bonds. Belize is issuing the New Bonds as part of its invitation to holders of Eligible Claims to tender their Eligible Claims for the New Bonds on the terms and subject to the conditions described in the offering memorandum dated December 18, 2006. Belize will not receive any cash proceeds from this invitation.

Amount of New Bonds Issued: $546,786,000.

Currency: The New Bonds will be denominated for purposes of both interest and principal in U.S. dollars.

Interest Rate: The New Bonds will accrue interest, payable semiannually in arrears, from February 20, 2007 at the interest rates per year set forth below:

From (and including)	To (but excluding)	Interest rate (per annum)
February 20, 2007	February 20, 2010	4.25 %
February 20, 2010	February 20, 2012	6.00 %
February 20, 2012	February 20, 2029	8.50 %

Interest Payment Dates: Each February 20 and August 20, commencing on August 20, 2007.

Final Maturity Date: February 20, 2029.

Amortizations: 20 equal semi-annual installments commencing August 20, 2019.

Optional Redemption: Belize may redeem the Securities at par together with accrued interest, in whole or in part, on any interest payment date falling on or after (but not prior to) August 20, 2019. Belize may at any time acquire (for cancellation) the New Bonds in the secondary market. See "Terms and Conditions of the New Bonds—Redemption" with respect to the New Bonds.

Modifications: The New Bonds will contain collective action clauses. See "Terms and Conditions of the New Bonds—Modifications" with respect to the New Bonds.

N. Gaillard, *When Sovereigns Go Bankrupt*, SpringerBriefs in Economics,
DOI 10.1007/978-3-319-08988-1

Ranking: The New Bonds will be general, direct, unconditional, unsubordinated and unsecured obligations of Belize, will rank equally with all of Belize's existing and future unsubordinated and unsecured Public Debt and will be backed by the full faith and credit of Belize.

Further Issuance: Belize may, from time to time, create and issue further bonds having the same terms as and ranking equally with the New Bonds in all respects and such further bonds will be consolidated and form a single series with the New Bonds.

Constitutive Document: The New Bonds will be issued under an indenture.

Withholding Tax: Belize will make all payments on the New Bonds without withholding or deducting any Belizean taxes, unless required by law. If Belizean law requires Belize to withhold or deduct taxes, Belize will pay holders of New Bonds, subject to certain exceptions, additional amounts to provide the equivalent of full payment to the holders. See "Terms and Conditions of the New Bonds—Taxation".

Negative Pledge Covenant: Belize may not create or suffer to exist any lien (with the exception of certain permitted liens) on its revenues or assets to secure Public Debt (as defined herein) unless Belize also causes such lien to secure equally and ratably the obligations of Belize with respect to the New Bonds.

Most Favored Creditor Undertaking: In the event that any single Eligible Claim (or portion thereof) representing 5 % or more of the aggregate amount of all Eligible Claims is not tendered in the Exchange Offer (each, an "Untendered Material Claim"), the New Bonds shall contain a covenant preventing Belize from entering into any arrangement to pay or to settle such an Untendered Material Claim on terms more favorable to the holder thereof (in a net present value sense) than the terms being offered herein to the holders of tendered Eligible Claims, without simultaneously making those more favorable terms available to each holder of a tendered Eligible Claim.

Events of Default; Acceleration: The following events, among others, shall be Events of Default under the New Bonds:

(i) Failure to pay any amount of interest or principal on the New Bonds (with a 30-day grace period);
(ii) Failure by Belize to observe or perform any of the other covenants or agreements provided herein or in the indenture (with a 60-day grace period);
(iii) Cross-acceleration of an aggregate principal amount of at least U.S.$25 million (or equivalent in other currencies) in respect of Public Debt issued, or amended as to payment terms, on or after the original issuance date of the New Bonds and such acceleration shall not have been rescinded or annulled;
(iv) Failure by Belize to satisfy, discharge, contest in good faith or obtain a stay of execution of any judgment against Belize or its assets (other than any such judgment rendered in respect of an Eligible Claim) for the payment of money exceeding U.S.$25 million within a period of 60 days;

(v) Invalidity of the New Bonds or the indenture; and
(vi) Failure to maintain membership in the International Monetary Fund (with a 60-day grace period).

Holders of 25 % or more of principal amount of the New Bonds may instruct the Trustee in writing to accelerate following the occurrence of an Event of Default.

Enforcement: Following the occurrence of an Event of Default, the power to enforce the New Bonds shall reside with the Trustee under the indenture, unless the Trustee shall have declined to exercise that power as provided in the indenture.

Governing Law: The New Bonds and the indenture will be governed by the law of the State of New York. Belize will submit to the jurisdiction of U.S. federal and New York State courts in New York City.

Restrictions on Resale: The New Bonds have not been registered under the U.S. Securities Act and will be subject to restrictions on resale under applicable law. See "Notice to Investors". The New Bonds will be subject to contractual transfer restrictions.

Listing: Belize intends to apply to admit the New Bonds to listing on the Luxembourg Stock Exchange and to trading on the Euro MTF market.

Denomination: New Bonds will be issued in denominations of U.S.$100 and higher integral multiples of U.S.$100 in excess thereof.

Form and Settlement: Belize will issue the New Bonds in the form of one or more fully registered global securities, without interest coupons attached, registered in the name of either a nominee for DTC [The Depository Trust Company] or a common depositary for Euroclear and Clearstream, as the case may be, and will deposit such global securities on or before the Closing Date with a custodian for DTC or a common depositary for Euroclear and Clearstream.

Trustee, Registrar, Transfer Agent and Paying Agent for New Bonds: The Bank of New York

Luxembourg Paying Agent and Transfer Agent: The Bank of New York (Luxembourg) S.A.

Luxembourg Listing Agent: Fortis Banque Luxembourg

Source: Belize (2007, pp. 7–9).

Appendix 3A: Letter of Intent from Ghana to the IMF, 2009

June 26, 2009

Mr. Dominique Strauss-Kahn
Managing Director
International Monetary Fund
Washington, DC 20431

Dear Mr. Strauss-Kahn:

After another peaceful, democratic and competitive election in Ghana in December 2008, a new government of the National Democratic Congress Party took over power in January 2009. The Government sees its political mandate as an opportunity to manage the economy to achieve prosperity for all Ghanaians.

While the country achieved significant gains in the macroeconomic and social areas through 2005, the last three years were characterized by severe imbalances brought on by external shocks that were compounded by expansionary domestic policies.

The new government is committed to addressing the economic imbalances, re-stabilizing the economy, and placing it on a path of sustained high growth in order to accelerate the pace of progress toward the Millennium Development Goals and middle income status for Ghana.

The attached Memorandum of Economic and Financial Policies (MEFP) reviews recent economic developments and policies, and outlines adjustment and reform policies intended under the program. In support of the policies in the MEFP, the government requests that the Executive Board of the IMF approve a Poverty Reduction and Growth Facility (PRGF) arrangement with access in the amount of SDR 387.45 million (105 percent of quota).

The Government of Ghana will provide such information as the Fund may request in connection with progress in implementing its economic and financial policies. The government believes that the policies set out in the attached MEFP are adequate to achieve the objectives of its program, but it will take any further measures that may become appropriate for this purpose. The Government will consult with the Fund on the adoption of these measures, and in advance of revisions to the policies contained in the MEFP, in accordance with the Fund's policies on such consultations.

Sincerely yours,

Dr. Kwabena Duffuor Minister of Finance and Economic Planning	Dr. Paul A. Acquah Governor Bank of Ghana

Source: IMF (2009, pp. 37–38).

N. Gaillard, *When Sovereigns Go Bankrupt*, SpringerBriefs in Economics,
DOI 10.1007/978-3-319-08988-1

Appendix 3B: IMF Conditionality for Ghana, 2009–2010

Measures	Timing	Macroeconomic rationale
I Prior actions		
Adoption of budget to limit fiscal deficit to 9.4 % of GDP in 2009	Implemented	A first step toward fiscal and debt sustainability
Adoption of measures yield at least 1.0 % of GDP to offset projected expenditure over-runs in the 2009 budget	Implemented	To preserve macroeconomic stability and avoid crowding out private sector credit
Selective public sector hiring freeze, with exemptions mainly limited to health and education trainees	Implemented	To strengthen control of the high and growing public payroll
Reinstatement of automatic bi-weekly price adjustments for petroleum products	Implemented	To eliminate energy subsidies
II Structural benchmarks		
Tax policy and revenue administration		
Complete comprehensive reviews of zero-rated VAT items and the nature and scope of tax exemptions and discretionary waivers	End September 2009	To strengthen revenue mobilization as part of the fiscal consolidation strategy
Cabinet approval of a modernization strategy for revenue administration	End December 2009	To strengthen revenue mobilization as part of the fiscal consolidation strategy
Public expenditure management		
Review of the effectiveness of the existing budget information management system, and decision on whether it should be modernized or replaced	End December 2009	To strengthen monitoring and control of budget execution

(continued)

N. Gaillard, *When Sovereigns Go Bankrupt*, SpringerBriefs in Economics,
DOI 10.1007/978-3-319-08988-1

Measures	Timing	Macroeconomic rationale
Public sector reform and payroll management		
Steps to strengthen oversight and control of public service recruitment and staffing	End September 2009	To strengthen oversight and control of the high and growing public payroll
Establish institutional responsibility for the restructuring, commercialization, or liquidation of subvented agencies	End December 2009	To promote fiscal savings by rationalizing subvented agency numbers
Monetary policy		
Adoption and launch of program to strengthen communication of framework for inflation targeting and disinflation over program period	End December 2009	To support the disinflation program

Source: IMF (2009, p. 57)

Appendix 4: Ratings Issued by Fitch, Moody's, S&P, and ECR Compared with 1-year and 10-year Bond Yields as of 14 January 2014

Country	Fitch rating	Moody's rating	S&P rating	ECR rating	1-year bond yield	10-year bond yield
Abu Dhabi	AA	Aa2	AA	N.R.	N.A.	N.A.
Albania	N.R.	B1	B	35.98	N.A.	N.A.
Angola	BB–	Ba3	BB–	39.85	N.A.	N.A.
Argentina	CC	B3	CCC+	30.22	N.A.	N.A.
Armenia	BB–	Ba2	N.R.	41.74	N.A.	N.A.
Aruba	BBB	N.R.	BBB+	N.R.	N.A.	N.A.
Australia	AAA	Aaa	AAA	81.05	2.530	4.241
Austria	AAA	Aaa	AA+	79.20	0.181	2.158
Azerbaijan	BBB–	Baa3	BBB–	45.84	N.A.	N.A.
Bahamas	N.R.	Baa1	BBB	53.63	N.A.	N.A.
Bahrain	BBB	Baa2	BBB	54.60	N.A.	N.A.
Bangladesh	N.R.	Ba3	BB–	31.96	N.A.	N.A.
Barbados	N.R.	Ba3	BB–	47.53	N.A.	N.A.
Belarus	N.R.	B3	B–	27.61	N.A.	N.A.
Belgium	AA	Aa3	AA	71.62	0.199	2.454
Belize	N.R.	Caa2	B–	37.89	N.A.	N.A.
Bermuda	AA–	Aa3	AA–	60.03	N.A.	N.A.
Bolivia	BB–	Ba3	BB–	38.91	N.A.	N.A.
Bosnia	N.R.	B3	B	23.04	N.A.	N.A.
Botswana	N.R.	A2	A–	54.10	N.A.	6.300
Brazil	BBB	Baa2	BBB	58.89	10.890	13.080
Bulgaria	BBB–	Baa2	BBB	51.14	0.799	3.588
Burkina Faso	N.R.	N.R.	B	37.12	N.A.	N.A.
Cambodia	N.R.	B2	B	22.57	N.A.	N.A.
Cameroon	B	N.R.	B	31.97	N.A.	N.A.

(continued)

N. Gaillard, *When Sovereigns Go Bankrupt*, SpringerBriefs in Economics,
DOI 10.1007/978-3-319-08988-1

Country	Fitch rating	Moody's rating	S&P rating	ECR rating	1-year bond yield	10-year bond yield
Canada	AAA	Aaa	AAA	81.62	0.950	2.580
Cape Verde	B+	N.R.	B	14.50	N.A.	N.A.
Chile	A+	Aa3	AA–	78.26	4.550	5.100
China	A+	Aa3	AA–	59.85	4.110	4.600
Colombia	BBB	Baa3	BBB	57.17	N.A.	6.670
Congo	B+	Ba3	B+	38.47	N.A.	N.A.
Costa Rica	BB+	Baa3	BB	47.79	N.A.	N.A.
Croatia	BB+	Ba1	BB+	49.31	1.430	5.203
Cuba	N.R.	Caa1	N.R.	19.72	N.A.	N.A.
Cyprus	B–	Caa3	B–	49.84	N.A.	N.A.
Czech Republic	A+	A1	AA–	68.64	0.140	2.500
Democratic Rep. of Congo	N.R.	B3	B–	31.84	N.A.	N.A.
Denmark	AAA	Aaa	AAA	83.19	0.210	1.882
Dominican Republic	B	B1	B+	35.38	N.A.	N.A.
Ecuador	B	Caa1	B	34.71	N.A.	N.A.
Egypt	B–	Caa1	B–	30.49	11.230	14.800
El Salvador	BB–	Ba3	BB–	41.59	N.A.	N.A.
Estonia	A+	A1	AA–	68.44	N.A.	N.A.
Fiji	N.R.	B1	B	20.88	N.A.	N.A.
Finland	AAA	Aaa	AAA	83.21	N.A.	2.019
France	AA+	Aa1	AA	70.25	0.209	2.476
Gabon	BB–	N.R.	BB–	45.88	N.A.	N.A.
Georgia	BB–	Ba3	BB–	40.42	N.A.	N.A.
Germany	AAA	Aaa	AAA	81.32	0.155	1.732
Ghana	B	B1	B	40.79	N.A.	N.A.
Greece	B–	Caa3	B–	32.54	N.A.	8.132
Grenada	N.R.	N.R.	SD	34.55	N.A.	N.A.
Guatemala	BB+	Ba1	BB	36.61	N.A.	N.A.
Honduras	N.R.	B2	B	34.62	N.A.	N.A.
Hong Kong	AA+	Aa1	AAA	79.41	0.240	2.389
Hungary	BB+	Ba1	BB	48.52	3.030	5.560
Iceland	BBB	Baa3	BBB–	58.69	N.A.	6.590
India	BBB–	Baa3	BBB–	50.74	8.870	8.712
Indonesia	BBB–	Baa3	BB+	49.56	7.470	8.640
Ireland	BBB+	Ba1	BBB+	58.66	0.300	3.300
Isle of Man	N.R.	Aa1	AA+	N.R.	N.A.	N.A.
Israel	A	A1	A+	66.14	0.960	3.698
Italy	BBB+	Baa2	BBB	54.56	0.747	3.884
Jamaica	CCC	Caa3	B–	30.99	N.A.	N.A.
Japan	A+	Aa3	AA–	67.12	0.081	0.658
Jordan	N.R.	B1	BB–	45.18	N.A.	N.A.

(continued)

Country	Fitch rating	Moody's rating	S&P rating	ECR rating	1-year bond yield	10-year bond yield
Kazakhstan	BBB+	Baa2	BBB+	50.81	N.A.	N.A.
Kenya	B+	B1	B+	35.64	10.65	11.990
Kuwait	AA	Aa2	AA	70.97	N.A.	N.A.
Latvia	BBB+	Baa2	BBB+	55.82	0.600	3.790
Lebanon	B	B1	B–	35.78	N.A.	N.A.
Lesotho	BB–	N.R.	N.R.	30.49	N.A.	N.A.
Lithuania	BBB+	Baa1	BBB	59.46	0.500	3.600
Luxembourg	AAA	Aaa	AAA	84.23	N.A.	N.A.
Macau	AA–	Aa3	N.R.	70.70	N.A.	N.A.
Macedonia	BB+	N.R.	BB–	38.79	N.A.	N.A.
Malaysia	A–	A3	A–	63.01	2.930	4.120
Malta	A	A3	BBB+	65.20	N.A.	N.A.
Mauritius	N.R.	Baa1	N.R.	47.58	3.970	N.A.
Mexico	BBB+	Baa1	BBB+	61.38	3.660	6.410
Moldova	N.R.	B3	N.R.	28.55	N.A.	N.A.
Mongolia	B+	B1	BB–	39.54	N.A.	N.A.
Montenegro	N.R.	Ba3	BB–	31.32	N.A.	N.A.
Morocco	BBB–	Ba1	BBB–	43.47	N.A.	N.A.
Mozambique	B+	B1	B+	33.99	N.A.	N.A.
Namibia	BBB–	Baa3	N.R.	54.11	N.A.	N.A.
Netherlands	AAA	Aaa	AA+	81.71	N.A.	2.127
New Zealand	AA	Aaa	AA	80.81	N.A.	4.710
Nicaragua	N.R.	B3	N.R.	27.17	N.A.	N.A.
Nigeria	BB–	Ba3	BB–	40.58	N.A.	N.A.
Norway	AAA	Aaa	AAA	89.79	1.388	N.A.
Oman	N.R.	A1	A	66.98	N.A.	N.A.
Pakistan	N.R.	Caa1	B–	30.29	10.060	12.600
Panama	BBB	Baa2	BBB	55.04	N.A.	N.A.
Papua New Guinea	N.R.	B1	B+	34.40	N.A.	N.A.
Paraguay	BB–	Ba3	BB–	40.54	N.A.	N.A.
Peru	BBB+	Baa2	BBB+	59.34	N.A.	N.A.
Philippines	BBB–	Baa1	BBB–	51.24	2.050	4.230
Poland	A–	A2	A–	66.63	2.652	4.366
Portugal	BB+	Ba3	BB	50.78	N.A.	5.310
Qatar	N.R.	Aa2	AA	76.23	N.A.	N.A.
Ras Al Khaimah	A	N.R.	A	N.R.	N.A.	N.A.
Romania	BBB–	Baa3	BB+	48.44	2.299	5.300
Russia	BBB	Baa1	BBB	54.53	5.900	7.770
Rwanda	B	N.R.	B	27.11	N.A.	N.A.
Saudi Arabia	AA–	Aa3	AA–	66.55	1.102	N.A.
Senegal	N.R.	B1	B+	35.60	N.A.	N.A.
Serbia	BB–	B1	BB–	39.19	N.A.	N.A.

(continued)

Country	Fitch rating	Moody's rating	S&P rating	ECR rating	1-year bond yield	10-year bond yield
Seychelles	B	N.R.	N.R.	38.93	N.A.	N.A.
Sharjah	N.R.	A3	A	N.R.	N.A.	N.A.
Singapore	AAA	Aaa	AAA	87.76	0.350	2.490
Slovakia	A+	A2	A	67.77	N.A.	N.A.
Slovenia	BBB+	Ba1	A–	57.79	N.A.	4.580
South Africa	BBB	Baa1	BBB	54.58	N.A.	7.950
South Korea	AA–	Aa3	A+	66.76	2.640	3.650
Spain	BBB	Baa3	BBB–	54.42	0.798	3.826
Sri Lanka	BB–	B1	B+	45.65	7.190	N.A.
St Vincent & the Grenadines	N.R.	B2	N.R.	35.04	N.A.	N.A.
Suriname	BB–	Ba3	BB–	38.83	N.A.	N.A.
Sweden	AAA	Aaa	AAA	82.94	N.A.	2.405
Switzerland	AAA	Aaa	AAA	88.51	0.080	1.217
Taiwan	A+	Aa3	AA–	74.73	N.A.	1.640
Thailand	BBB+	Baa1	BBB+	53.92	2.350	4.030
Trinidad & Tobago	N.R.	Baa1	A	57.36	N.A.	N.A.
Tunisia	BB–	Ba3	N.R.	40.69	N.A.	N.A.
Turkey	BBB–	Baa3	BB+	55.79	9.450	9.830
Uganda	B	B1	B+	33.94	12.250	14.47
Ukraine	B–	Caa1	B–	32.01	12.200	N.A.
United Arab Emirates	N.R.	Aa2	N.R.	68.84	N.A.	N.A.
United Kingdom	AA+	Aa1	AAA	71.52	0.401	2.836
United States	AAA	Aaa	AA+	74.75	0.112	2.869
Uruguay	BBB–	Baa3	BBB–	54.89	N.A.	N.A.
Venezuela	B+	Caa1	B–	29.06	N.A.	N.A.
Vietnam	B+	B2	BB–	40.04	6.460	8.890
Zambia	B	B1	B+	35.42	N.A.	N.A.

Sources: fitchratings.com, moodys.com, standardandpoors.com, euromoneycountryrisk.com, and investing.com
Notes: *N.R.* not rated, *N.A.* not available

Bibliography

Abreu M de P, de Souza FCL (2011) 'Palatable Foreign Control': British money doctors and central banking in South America, 1924–1935. Texto para discussão No. 597. Departamento de Economia, Pontifical Catholic University of Rio de Janeiro

Adamson MR (2002) The failure of the Foreign Bondholders Protective Council experiment, 1934–1940. Bus Hist Rev 76(3)

AIG (2006) Political risk insurance. AIG, New York

Alacevich M, Asso PF (2009) Money doctoring after World War II: Arthur I. Bloomfield and the Federal Reserve missions to South Korea. Hist Polit Econ 41(2)

Arab Republic of Egypt (2007) LE 6,000,000,000 8.75% notes due 2012 – issue price 99.504% – payable in U.S. dollars, 16 July

Arora V, Cerisola M (2001) How does U.S. monetary policy influence sovereign spreads in emerging markets? IMF Staff Pap 48(3)

Avendaño R, Gaillard N, Nieto-Parra S (2011) Are workers' remittances relevant for credit rating agencies? Rev Dev Financ 1(1)

Baldacci E, Gupta S, Mati A (2008) Is it (still) mostly fiscal? Determinants of sovereign spreads in emerging markets. IMF working paper no. 08/259

Bank for International Settlements [BIS] (1936, 1937) Annual report. Basel

Bank for International Settlements [BIS] (2013) Statistical release: OTC derivatives statistics at end-December 2012. Monetary and Economic Department, Basel

Belize (2007) $546,786,000 – U.S. dollar bonds due 2029, 5 Mar

Blanchard O, Leigh D (2013) Growth forecast errors and fiscal multipliers. IMF working paper no. 13/1

Borchard E (1951) State insolvency and foreign bondholders. General principles, vol I. Yale University Press, New Haven

Bordo M, Rockoff H (1996) The gold standard as a good housekeeper seal of approval. J Econ Hist 56(2)

Bordo MD, Meissner CM, Stuckler D (2010) Foreign currency debt, financial crises and economic growth: a long-run view. J Int Money Financ 29(4)

Boughton JM (2001) Silent revolution: the International Monetary Fund, 1979–1989. International Monetary Fund, Washington, DC

Brau E, McDonald I (eds) (2009) Successes of the International Monetary Fund – untold stories of cooperation at work. Palgrave Macmillan, New York

Brownlie I (2003) Principles of public international law. Oxford University Press, Oxford

Buchheit LC, Pam JS (2004) The pari passu clause in sovereign debt instruments. Emory Law J 53 (Special edition)

N. Gaillard, *When Sovereigns Go Bankrupt*, SpringerBriefs in Economics,
DOI 10.1007/978-3-319-08988-1

Campbell JY, Shiller RJ (1996) A scorecard for indexed government debt. In: Bernanke BS, Rotemberg JJ (eds) NBER macroeconomics annual 1996, vol 11. MIT Press, Cambridge
Cantor R, Packer F (1996) Determinants and impacts of sovereign credit ratings. Economic Policy Review, Federal Reserve Bank of New York, October
Cantor R, Ap Gwilym O, Thomas SH (2007) The use of credit ratings in investment management in the U.S. and Europe. J Fixed Income 17(2)
Canuto O, Liu L (eds) (2013) Until debt do us part – subnational debt, insolvency, and markets. World Bank, Washington, DC
Choi SJ, Gulati M, Posner EA (2012) The evolution of contractual terms in sovereign bonds. J Legal Anal 4(1)
Citi (2013) Sovereign default risk and relative value. Citi Research, Multi-Asset, 24 Dec
Clark JR (1940) Collecting on defaulted foreign dollar bonds. Am J Int Law 31(1)
Cohen RA (2011) Sometimes a cigar is just a cigar: the simple story of pari passu. Hofstra Law Rev 40(1)
Committee on Foreign and Comparative Law (2013) Governing law in sovereign debt – lessons from the Greek crisis and Argentina dispute of 2012. Working paper, Feb
Corporation of Foreign Bondholders [CFB] (1874, 1878, 1895, 1904, 1907, 1943) Annual report. Council of Corporation of Foreign Bondholders, London
Cruces JJ, Trebesch C (2011) Sovereign defaults: the price of haircuts. CESifo working paper no. 3604, Oct
Das US, Papaioannou MG, Trebesch C (2012) Sovereign debt restructurings 1950–2010: literature survey, data, and stylized facts. IMF working paper no. 12/203
Decorzant Y, Flores JH (2012) Public borrowing in harsh times: the League of Nations loans revisited. Working Papers in Economic History WP 12-07. Universidad Carlos III de Madrid
Delaume GR (1957) Jurisdiction of courts and international loans. A study of lenders' practice. Am J Comp Law 6(2/3)
Delaume GR (1994) The Foreign Sovereign Immunities Act and public debt litigation: some fifteen years later. Am J Int Law 88(2)
Deutsche Bank (2013) Where is the FX 'pain threshold'? Global Markets Research – Macro 25 Jan
Diaz-Cassou J, Erce-Dominguez A, Vazquez-Zamora JJ (2008) Recent episodes of sovereign debt restructurings. A case-study approach. Documentos Ocasionales No. 0804. Banco de España
Dornbusch R, Draghi M (eds) (1990) Public debt management: theory and history. Cambridge University Press, Cambridge/New York
Edwards S (1984) LDC foreign borrowing and default risk: an empirical investigation, 1976–80. Am Econ Rev 74(4)
Eichengreen B, Gupta P (2013) Tapering talk: the impact of expectations of reduced Federal Reserve security purchases on emerging markets. World Bank working paper manuscript. 12 Dec
Eichengreen B, Sachs J (1985) Exchange rates and economic recovery in the 1930s. J Econ Hist 45(4)
Eichengreen B, Hausmann R, Panizza U (2005a) The pain of original sin. In: Eichengreen B, Hausmann R (eds) Other people's money. Chicago University Press, Chicago
Eichengreen B, Hausmann R, Panizza U (2005b) The mystery of original sin. In: Eichengreen B, Hausmann R (eds) Other people's money. Chicago University Press, Chicago
Enderlein H, Trebesch C, Von Daniels L (2012) Sovereign debt disputes: A database on government coerciveness during debt crises. J Int Money Financ 31(2)
Eurogroup (2012) Eurogroup statement, 21 Feb
Fischer Williams J (1925) Le droit international et les obligations financières internationales qui naissent d'un contrat. Recueil des cours 1923 – Académie de droit international de La Haye. Hachette, Paris

Fishlow A (1989) Conditionality and willingness to pay: some parallels from the 1890s. In: Eichengreen B, Lindert PH (eds) The international debt crisis in historical perspective. MIT Press, Cambridge/London

Flandreau M, Zumer F (2004) The making of global finance – 1880–1913. Development centre studies. OECD, Paris

Flandreau M, Flores JH, Gaillard N, Nieto-Parra S (2010) The end of gatekeeping: underwriters and the quality of sovereign bond markets, 1815–2007. In: Reichlin L, West K (eds) NBER international seminar on macroeconomics 2009. NBER and University of Chicago Press, Chicago

Flandreau M, Gaillard N, Packer F (2011) To err is human: US rating agencies and the interwar foreign government debt crisis. Eur Rev Econ Hist 15(3)

Foreign Bondholders Protective Council [FBPC] (1945) Report 1941 through 1944. Foreign Bondholders Protective Council, New York

Gaillard N (2011) A century of sovereign ratings. Springer, New York

Gaillard N (2014a) What is the value of sovereign ratings? Ger Econ Rev 15(1)

Gaillard N (2014b) How and why credit rating agencies missed the Eurozone debt crisis. Cap Market Law J 9(2)

Garbowski M (2008) Credit default swaps: a brief insurance primer. Anderson Kill & Olick Policyholder Advisor 17(3), September/October

Gelpern A, Gulati M (2006) Public symbol in private contract: a case study. Wash Univ Law Rev 84(7)

Gille B (1965) Histoire de la Maison Rothschild – Volume I: des origines à 1848. Droz, Geneva

Glaser E (2003) Chile's monetarist money doctors, 1850–1988. In: Flandreau M (ed) Money doctors – the experience of international financial advising 1850–2000. Routledge, London/New York

Guitian M (1995) Conditionality: past, present, future. IMF Staff Pap 42(4)

Gulati M, Klee KN (2001) Sovereign piracy. University of California, Los Angeles School of Law Research paper no. 01-7

Hartelius K, Kashiwase K, Kodres LE (2008) Emerging market spread compression: is it real or is it liquidity? IMF working paper no 08/10

Harvey CR (1993) Term structure forecasts economic growth. Finan Anal J 49(3)

Hemerijck A (2013) Changing welfare states. Oxford University Press, Oxford

Independent Evaluation Group (2009) The World Bank Group guarantee instruments 1990–2007. An independent evaluation. World Bank, Washington, DC

International Monetary Fund [IMF] (2002) Collective action clauses in sovereign bond contracts – encouraging greater use. Policy Development and Review, International Capital Markets and Legal Departments, 6 June

International Monetary Fund [IMF] (2009) Ghana: 2009 article IV consultation and request for a three-year arrangement under the poverty reduction and growth facility—staff report; staff supplement; staff statement; public information notice and press release on the executive board discussion; and statement by the executive director for Ghana. IMF country report no. 09/256

International Monetary Fund [IMF] (2010) IMF executive board cancels Haiti's debt and approves new three-year program to support reconstruction and economic growth. Press release no. 10/299 21, July 2010

International Monetary Fund [IMF] (2013a) Global financial stability report – old risks, new challenges. International Monetary Fund, Washington, DC

International Monetary Fund [IMF] (2013b) Greece: ex post evaluation of exceptional access under the 2010 stand-by arrangement. IMF country report no. 13/156

International Monetary Fund [IMF] (2013c) Annual report. International Monetary Fund, Washington, DC

International Monetary Fund [IMF] (2014) IMF conditionality, 31 Mar

Johnson O, Salop J (1980) Distributional aspects of stabilization programs in developing countries. IMF Staff Pap 27(1)

Jorgensen E, Sachs J (1989) Default and renegotiation of Latin American foreign bonds in the interwar period. In: Eichengreen B, Lindert PH (eds) The international debt crisis in historical perspective. MIT Press, Cambridge/London
Kaminsky G, Reinhart C, Végh C (2003) The unholy trinity of financial contagion. J Econ Perspect 17(4)
Kaufmann D, Kraay A, Mastruzzi M (2010) The worldwide governance indicators: a summary of methodology, data and analytical issues. World Bank Policy Research working paper no. 5430
Kemmerer EW (1927) Economic advisory work for governments. Am Econ Rev 17(1)
Koeberle S, Bedoya H, Silarszky P, Verheyen G (eds) (2005) Conditionality revisited – concepts, experiences, and lessons. World Bank, Washington, DC
Lebanese Republic (2009) U.S.$22,000,000,000 – the Lebanese Republic global medium-term note program, 26 Feb
Lindert PH, Morton PJ (1989) How sovereign debt has worked. In: Sachs J (ed) Developing country debt and economic performance. The international financial system, vol 1. University of Chicago Press, Chicago
Lipson C (1981) The international organization of third world debt. Int Organ 35(4)
Löffler G (2004) An anatomy of rating through the cycle. J Bank Financ 28(3)
Ludington S, Gulati M, Brophy AL (2010) Applied legal history: demystifying the doctrine of odious debts. Theor Inq Law 11(1)
Mattlin M, Nojonen M (2011) Conditionality in Chinese bilateral lending. BOFIT discussion papers 14/2011. Bank of Finland, Institute for Economies in Transition, Helsinki
Mauro P, Sussman N, Yafeh Y (2002) Emerging market spreads: then versus now. Q J Econ 117(2)
Mintz I (1951) Deterioration in the quality of foreign bonds issued in the United States 1920–30. NBER, Cambridge
Mitchener KJ, Weidenmier MD (2005) Supersanctions and sovereign debt repayment. NBER working paper no. 11472
Mitchener KJ, Weidenmier MD (2007) The Baring crisis and the great Latin American meltdown of the 1890s. NBER working paper no. 13403
Moody's Investors Service (2007) Moody's explains why wealthiest Gulf States are not rated Aaa, 7 Nov
Moody's Investors Service (2013a) Sovereign default and recovery rates, 1983–2012, 12 June
Moody's Investors Service (2013b) Sovereign bond ratings, 12 Sept
Moody's Investors Service (1922, 1924, 1929, 1937) Moody's manual of investments – American and foreign government securities. Moody's Investors Service, New York
Moreau E (1954) Souvenirs d'un Gouverneur de la Banque de France. Editions M.-Th. Génin, Paris
Multilateral Investment Guarantee Agency [MIGA] (2012) Annual report 2012. Multilateral Investment Guarantee Agency, Washington, DC
Neiss H, Tseng W, Gordon J (2009) The Korean crisis ten years later: a success story. In: Brau E, McDonald I (eds) Successes of the International Monetary Fund – untold stories of cooperation at work. Palgrave Macmillan, New York
Obstfeld M, Taylor A (2003) Sovereign risk, credibility and the gold standard: 1870–1913 versus 1925–31. Econ J 113(487)
Organization for Economic Co-operation and Development (2010) Tax policy reform and economic growth. OECD tax policy studies no. 20
Pack AJ (1932) Economic conditions in Chile. Department of Overseas Trade, London
Packer F, Suthiphongchai C (2003) Sovereign credit default swaps. BIS Quarterly Review, Dec
Panizza U, Sturzenegger F, Zettelmeyer J (2009) The economics and law of sovereign debt and default. J Econ Lit 47(3)
Polak JJ (1991) The changing nature of IMF conditionality. Essay in international finance no. 184. Department of Economics. Princeton University, Princeton
Polanyi K (1944) The great transformation. Beacon Press, Boston
Rancière R (2002) Credit derivatives in emerging markets. IMF policy discussion paper, Apr

Reinhart C (2012) The return of financial repression. Financial Stability Review, Banque de France, no. 16

Reinhart C, Rogoff K (2009) This time is different – eight centuries of financial folly. Princeton University Press, Princeton

Reinhart C, Rogoff K, Savastano M (2003) Debt intolerance. NBER working paper no. 9908

Reisen H, von Maltzan J (1999) Boom and bust and sovereign ratings. OECD Development Centre working paper no. 148

Republic of El Salvador (2011) US$653,500,000 – 7.625% notes due 2041, 25 Jan

Republic of Ghana (2007) US$750,000,000 8.5% – notes due 2017 – issue price: 100%, 2 Oct

Republic of Paraguay (2013) US$500,000,000 4.625% bonds due 2023, 17 Jan

Republic of the Philippines (2003) US$750,000,000 8.25% global bonds due 2014, 15 July

Robinson LR (1929) Investment trust organization and management. Ronald Press, New York

Rosenberg ES (1999) Financial missionaries to the world: the politics and culture of dollar diplomacy, 1900–1930. Harvard University Press, Cambridge

Rosenberg ES, Rosenberg NL (1987) From colonialism to professionalism: the public-private dynamic in United States foreign financial advising, 1898–1929. J Am Hist 74(1)

Rowland P, Torres JL (2004) Determinants of spread and creditworthiness for emerging market sovereign debt: a panel data study. Banco de la República, Colombia, Borrador de Economía 295

Sachs J (1986) Managing the LDC debt crisis. Brook Pap Econ Act 1986 (2)

Sachs J (1988) Comprehensive debt retirement: the Bolivian example. Brook Pap Econ Act 1988 (2)

Sachs J (1989) Strengthening IMF programs in highly indebted countries. In: Gwin C, Feinberg R (eds) The International Monetary Fund in a multipolar world: pulling together. U.S.-third world policy perspectives no. 13. Transaction Books, New Brunswick

Sack AN (1927) Les effets des transformations des Etats sur leurs dettes publiques et autres obligations financières. Sirey, Paris

Schmitthoff M (1937) The international government loan. J Comp Legis Int Law Third Ser 19(4)

Schuker SA (2003) Money doctors between the wars. In: Flandreau M (ed) Money doctors – the experience of international financial advising 1850–2000. Routledge, London/New York

Sgard J (2012) The IMF meets commercial banks: sovereign debt restructuring between 1970 and 1989. Sciences Po/CERI manuscript

Shaw CS (2005) Rothschilds and Brazil: an introduction to sources in the Rothschild archive. Lat Am Res Rev 40(1)

Smithson C, Mengle D (2006) The promise of credit derivatives in nonfinancial corporations (and why it's failed to materialize). J Appl Corp Financ 18(4)

Standard & Poor's (2006) Default study: sovereign defaults at 26-year low, to show little change in 2007, 18 Sept

Standard & Poor's (2013) Sovereign government rating methodology and assumptions, 24 June

Stiglitz JE (2002) Globalization and its discontents. W. W. Norton, New York/London

Stumpf MH (2010) Reflections on the Bosnia debt restructuring. Law Contemp Probl 73 Fall

Suter C, Stamm H (1992) Coping with global debt crises: debt settlements, 1820 to 1986. Comp Stud Soc Hist 34(4)

Taracouzio TA (1935) The Soviet Union and international law. MacMillan, New York

Ukraine (2012) US$1,250,000,000 7.8 per cent – notes due 2022 – issue price: 100 per cent, 26 Nov

Waibel M (2011) Sovereign defaults before international courts and tribunals. Cambridge University Press, Cambridge

Weidemaier MC (2010) Contracting for state intervention: the origins of sovereign debt arbitration. Law Contemp Probl 73 Fall

Weidemaier MC (2014) Sovereign immunity and sovereign debt. Univ Ill Law Rev 2014(1)

Weidemaier MC, Gulati M (2012) A people's history of collective action clauses. UNC Legal Studies Research paper no. 2172302

Weiss MA (2006) Iraq's debt relief: procedure and potential implications for international debt relief. CRS report for congress, 21 Apr

Williamson J (1990) What Washington means by policy reform. In: Williamson J (ed) Latin American adjustment: how much has happened? Peterson Institute for International Economics, Washington, DC

Winkler M (1933) Foreign bonds – an autopsy. Roland Swain, Philadelphia

World Economic Forum [WEF] (2004) The global competitiveness report 2004–2005. World Economic Forum, Geneva

World Economic Forum [WEF] (2009) The global competitiveness report 2009–2010. World Economic Forum, Geneva

Wynne WH (1951) State insolvency and foreign bondholders, vol II. Yale University Press, New Haven

Zurich (2009) Non-honoring of sovereign guarantee insurance. Zurich, Washington, DC

MIX
Papier aus verantwortungsvollen Quellen
Paper from responsible sources
FSC® C105338
FSC
www.fsc.org

If you have any concerns about our products,
you can contact us on
ProductSafety@springernature.com

In case Publisher is established outside the EU,
the EU authorized representative is:
Springer Nature Customer Service Center GmbH
Europaplatz 3, 69115 Heidelberg, Germany

Printed by Libri Plureos GmbH
in Hamburg, Germany